Gimblett's Guide to the B
Published in Great Britai
1st Edition publ

Jeroboam Press
Jeroboam House, Sandy Lane, Grayswood
Haslemere, Surrey, GU27 2DG

For Pamela, ever my guide.

There are many people I wish to thank for their assistance in preparing the guide. Foremost I would like to thank the talented Andrew Till of Studio Moka who offered to design the guide for fun, just because he loves cheese. And it is testament to that passion, as it turned out to be a task greater than either of us expected.

I would like to thank Eric Wood, our business consultant, for his generous counsel and enthusiasm for the project. I am grateful to Jonathan Andrews, whose editorial eye helped to bring order to my writing. Thanks also to dairy consultant Paul Thomas, for helping cheese-edit the guide as well as for mentoring Pam and me in our cheesemaking over the years.

I value the generosity of the time I spent with Iain and Rory Mellis of I.J Mellis, Hero Hirsh of Paxton and Whitfield, David Lockwood at Neal's Yard Dairy, Andy Swinscoe of The Courtyard Dairy and Ed Goodman of The Cheese Stall, all of whom provided considerable depth of knowledge in the complexities of bringing the finest artisan cheese to people's cheeseboards. My thanks also to Sian Oliver-Gay and the team the fabulous Specialist Cheesemakers Association for research on my behalf. Lizzie Patterson's photography for the introductory pages I would also like to highlight, as to step from fashion and portrait photography for a day tiptoeing through cow manure would be more than most as highly sought after a photographer might consider.

Finally, I would like to thank every cheesemaker in this guide as well as their colleagues that I met on my tour around Britain. I would like to thank them not only for helping me with information, samples, the occasional meal and even shelter, but moreover for producing a product that would not be in existence without a considerable amount of passion and love. The fabrication of artisan cheese is not a pursuit for those chasing riches.

INTRODUCTION

The initial idea and the eventual creation of this guide diverged from almost the moment I started my research on a blustery afternoon late in 2018. I thought I could write the content from the comfort of my office, using the time afforded by our dairy refurbishment to make a few calls to interview cheesemakers and catalogue my favourite British cheeses. It would be a guide book for artisan cheese lovers, something uniquely British and easily digestible that could be dipped into. I'd buy cheese samples from local delicatessens, and what I couldn't find I'd buy online. Simple; a bit of productive fun that could fill the time between our tasting events now our hands weren't curd-covered. What was to come would mature my callow view of the state of British artisan cheese, my desires as a cheesemaker, as well as set me on a quest that I'm still by no means certain I have the resources or the ability to complete.

Pam (my wife and fellow cheesemaker) and I started compiling a list of British artisan cheeses. Our event favourites were the first noted, totalling just shy of thirty cheeses. This was doable. Out came the books. The essential *Cheese* by Patricia Michaelson, and Juliet Harbutt's weighty *World Encyclopedia of Cheese*, amongst others, added to their number. Three hundred and thirty, all worthy of consideration. I had read, and for some time been expounding, that Britain, remarkably, had more styles of cheese than France. Just how many more were out there? I visited the websites of all the cheesemakers on my list to add their other offerings. I was up to nearly five hundred. This was now more daunting than exciting. Another two weeks of research, including a trawl of the fabulous Specialist Cheesemakers Association website, racked up another two hundred and sixty artisan cheeses – those made in a traditional or non-mechanised way from high quality milk. (There were plenty more commercial brands.) This was turning into an unachievable brief. I needed to prioritise. I decided I would only include those I considered to be of the highest quality; but how could I begin to adjudicate, without tasting, which cheeses would be most worthy of entry?

Taste and quality in cheese derive from several factors. The structure and aromatic diversity of the finest artisan cheeses are largely dependent upon the source material, the milk from which they are made, and therein lie clues to quality such as low yields (leading to concentration of character), individual herds or flocks (leading to particularity of flavour), minimal intervention (reducing damage to structural and aromatic potential) and whether they are farm-produced (greater ability to govern milk quality for cheesemaking). Scoring the cheeses based on these factors gave me a scale I could further refine. In the end I settled upon a list of just over three hundred cheeses, an ample snapshot of the top end of our industry. Coincidentally, they equated to one hundred cheesemakers.

By this point I had realised that to taste the cheeses as each cheesemaker intended I would need to get them from source. Moreover, to be able to tell each cheesemaker's story with a sense of their setting, the interview would need to be staged in situ. It was November. Aware that we wanted to resume cheesemaking in the spring, and that our events would pick up then too, I gave myself one hundred days to visit the one hundred cheesemakers on my final list, something that would inoculate my research with a serum of urgency. My enthusiasm riding high, I looked at the finances for the trip. I was mortified. Accommodation costs put the plan firmly into the realm of fantasy travel, and the fuel alone would likely be more than any royalties I might receive. Undeterred, I resolved to camp in the roof tent of my Land Rover and, should I earn enough to cover the cost of my fuel, then I would deem the trip a success. Sometimes, I mused, fantasy should trump reality.

The entries in this guide are all of cheesemakers I visited, and all the cheeses were tasted at the dairy, or under cover of canvas within a day or two of the visit. Not all the cheesemakers I visited are in this guide but I am pleased to say that I have since discovered cheesemakers who will be worthy of entry in a second edition further to a future visit.

Francis Gimblett

ABOUT THE AUTHOR

Francis lives in Haslemere at the northern tip of the South Downs National Park, making cheese and running online and live tastings with wife and co-cheesemaker, Pam.

Following training as a chef, Francis became the country's youngest sommelier at a five-star hotel, a year after he was legally entitled to drink. He became head sommelier a year later. After subsequent periods in fine wine broking and then winemaking overseas he formed Taste of the Vine, a company that has staged over 3000 wine, cheese, whisky, ale, cider and other fermentation-based tasting events in 47 countries over 23 years. In 2014, the passion for cheese overtook others and he and wife Pam started Gimblett Cheese after two years research and trials. Starting with a washed-rind cheese modelled on the output of ancient monasteries, the company is now developing a new Sussex cheese in the British Heritage mould to assist the Campaign for British Artisan Cheese.

TASTE THE GUIDE

Visit Francis and Pam's website for details of cheesemaking, public and private events and individual tasting packs covering fermented produce, including the finest of the guide's artisan cheeses, as well as international wines, miro-brewery ales, single malt whiskies and small-grower ciders.

CHEESEMAKING, TASTING PACKS, PUBLIC EVENTS, CAMPAIGN:
WWW.GIMBLETTCHEESE.CO.UK

CORPORATE TASTINGS: WWW.TASTEOFTHEVINE.CO.UK

NOTES ON THE GUIDE

The list of cheeses for a cheesemaker is sometimes a selection only, those that were put forward to best represent their range. Some ranges include other cheeses that would have been worthy of inclusion.

TASTING NOTES

Having worked with wine since my late teens, and hosting tasting events of fermented drinks and food for the last twenty-five years, I have developed a method of writing tasting notes that uses reference aromatics to remind me about what I have tasted. I believe that this is all a tasting note should be, not an absolute statement as to exactly what another should experience, as the detection of aromatic compounds by the olfactory system (as aroma via the nose or flavour via the palate) is subjective and influenced by personal experience. If you grew up with a gooseberry bush in your garden, you'll likely be more sensitive to its scent and be able to articulate the smell if you encounter it in a drink, such as New Zealand sauvignon, that shares similar aromatic compounds.

We are all able, unless we have a condition like anosmia (the loss of your sense of smell), to detect aromatics to similar levels. The practice of articulating what you taste comes with a little practice. Even so, it will always remain subjective. That said, high quality artisan cheeses will generally exhibit a greater range of aromatics than mass-produced cheeses, and the best of artisan cheeses will have persistent and changing aromas that prompt the taster to explore the frontal lobe's reference library to the full. The aromatic compounds in these finer cheeses are created by complex enzymes, which are in turn generated by the complex microflora within the milk and the environment the cheese is matured in. This is the reason you will never see florid tasting notes for highly processed cheeses made with a small range of dominant cultures and sealed from external influences during their maturation in plastic wrap. I happily admit that commercial Cheddar rarely lasts long in our house; like a house wine, it's a great staple but not one worthy of lengthy contemplation.

SCORING

When tasting the cheeses, I scored them using a 100-point scale converted from the wine scoring system I use, based upon the Wine Spectator's 100 point scale. Each cheese is given a score out of ten for each of the following: rind appearance, core appearance, rind nose, core nose, core taste, rind taste, and up to forty points for overall quality. To score a bottle of wine is relevant, as a vintage year can be stated and all bottles of the same vintage year will taste, more-or-less, as the taster scored it. To score a cheese for publication is not useful, unless the same day's make (the equivalent of a wine vintage) is the one being purchased and only if it is purchased within a day or two of when the score was given (as cheeses alter at a much faster rate than wines). In short, it is a practical impossibility. However, with a desire to indicate which cheeses for me shone on their day, I have named cheeses gaining 90-100 points as exceptional and 80-90 points as outstanding. All other cheeses included in the guide were good or very good.

QUALITY ASSURANCE

There exists little quality assurance labelling in the British artisan cheese world, namely designations indicating that a cheese is, for instance, handmade, made from superior milk, or to a traditional recipe. Many producers I met believe this is a factor inhibiting consumer understanding and therefore an inclination to select a more expensive cheese, particularly when on a supermarket shelf or similar environment where the 'risk' of spending a little more on an unfamiliar cheese rests entirely with them.

To this end I have indicated the elements I consider to be key factors contributing to quality. It does not follow however that because a cheese is made on a dairy farm, it will be of higher quality than one made from purchased milk, nor will a cheese made from unpasteurised milk necessarily be superior to one made from pasteurised milk. However, it is my belief that, on the basis of potential quality, if an artisan cheesemaker were offered the option to make their cheese on-farm, from the milk of a single herd of small-breed cattle, sheep, goats or buffalo, unpasteurised and to an artisan recipe involving traditional, minimal-intervention methods, they would choose to do so, commercial and practical considerations notwithstanding.

SINGLE HERD OR FLOCK

The fence symbol indicates that the milk for the cheese originated from a single herd of cows, goats, buffalo, or a flock of sheep grazed or housed in the same location. The milk may have been made into cheese on farm or purchased by a creamery. Although milk from a single source is no guarantee of greater quality, it can be a conduit to more particularity of flavour (akin to 'single vineyard' in wines). For instance, the forage of a single herd will have a distinct impact upon the structure of, and microflora within, the milk and the resulting flavour of the cheese. Cheeses made from the combined milk of many herds will have a more homogenous base from which flavour can derive.

SMALL BREED

Rather than being a reference to an animal's particular size, these symbols denote milk originating from breeds not bred or cross-bred for their capacity to produce high volumes of milk for the bulk milk market. For the purpose of this guide all breeds of sheep and goat fall into this category. For cows, they would typically produce less than 8,000 litres of milk per year each.

Commonly encountered small breeds of cow in British cheesemaking are:

British:	Ayrshire, Gloucester, Guernsey, Jersey, Shorthorn, Red Poll.
Other:	Brown Swiss, Buffalo, Fleckvieh, Friesian, Meuse-Rhine-Issel, Montbéliarde, Normandy, Norwegian Red, Simmental, Swedish Red, Viking Red.

BRITISH HERITAGE STYLE

This symbol denotes the styles of cheese considered native to Britain: 'territorial' cheeses that have evolved over the centuries to suit our farming systems, climate, geography and market requirements. Examples of such cheeses are traditional cloth-bound Cheddar or Red Leicester, or 'crumblies' such as Lancashire and Cheshire, the best examples of which are now only made in tiny volumes when compared to the inert incarnations bearing their names on most supermarket shelves.

HAND MADE

All the cheeses in this guide fall within this category. The symbol denotes a cheese made without significant mechanical processes or intervention. I visited a small number of large creameries using high levels of mechanisation. Based upon my tasting notes and scores, I felt unable to include their cheeses.

ON FARM

On farm indicates a cheese that was made where the milk originated. Again, whilst not a guarantee of superior quality on its own, it can be a clue that milk production is geared towards cheesemaking. It also assists the cheesemaker's task to obtain milk that is as fresh as possible, a factor particularly important with unpasteurised cheeses. There are, however, cheesemakers transporting cheesemaking-grade milk from small farms and producing both exceptional unpasteurised and pasteurised cheeses.

UNPASTEURISED

In the guide you will find cheeses made with pasteurised as well as unpasteurised milk. The process of pasteurisation is used to eliminate potential pathogens, such as Listeria, E-coli and Salmonella, as well as spoiler bacteria from milk. Outbreaks of illness from cheeses made from unpasteurised milk are extremely rare, especially when compared to cases of illness caused by other food-borne sources, such as Campylobacter from chicken. Also, in many cases contamination in cheese occurs post-pasteurisation in production, some would say because the cheese has lost its natural microflora that would otherwise protect the milk or cheese. In some instances, milk may be required to be pasteurised if there is an issue with bovine tuberculosis in a herd, though most milk is pasteurised simply to provide a more consistent base for the cheesemaker to work with, lessening the potential for variation from batch to batch. The process of pasteurisation can take place at 71.7°C for at least 15 seconds (referred to as HTST, High Temperature, Short Time) or at 63°C for thirty minutes (LTLT, Low Temperature, Long Time), the latter often referred to as vat pasteurisation. Unlike much higher temperature methods, such as for sterilised milk (120°C for 30 minutes), in pasteurised milk some microflora remains, which will in part influence the character of the final cheese. Thermisation, a gentler form of heat treatment, takes place at 63°C for 15 seconds and, for regulatory purposes, milk and cheese treated this way is considered unpasteurised and often labelled as such. These are not the same as raw milk cheeses which undergo no form of heat treatment other than the temperature at which the cheese would naturally be made. If the animals are healthy, the milk handling processes clean, and the cheese made with a careful understanding of handling raw milk, there is little risk from eating raw milk cheese.

UNPASTEURISED VS. PASTEURISED

A debate rages within the artisan cheese world between those who believe that unpasteurised milk is better for cheesemaking because pasteurisation kills the natural microflora and destroys natural enzymes that impart individuality in cheese, and those who say it makes little difference, pointing to pasteurised cheeses that are as flavourful and as good as unpasteurised ones. I believe both views are fair. If you strive to express a 'taste of place', where milk microflora has been least affected by artificial processes, then unpasteurised milk better suits that aim. In cheeses made from pasteurised milk, the structure of the milk and the natural microflora and enzymes that have survived pasteurisation will still play some part in instilling a taste of place and, in the hands of a skilled cheesemaker, such a cheese can still be delicious, have wide ranging flavours and be just as high quality as an unpasteurised one.

Some cheeses are made with starter cultures cultivated using only the lactic acid bacteria found wild within the milk of a herd or flock. A purist practitioner of unpasteurised milk and taste of place might well say that the milk should not be influenced by purchased culture additions at all but made only with the lactic acid bacteria naturally occurring in the milk and ripened only by cultures already in the milk and in the immediate environment. Such cheeses are rare in Britain, as they alter and respond to changes in environment in an even more marked way than unpasteurised ones. This all demands greater skill from a cheesemaker, as well as a sympathetic cheesemonger willing to allow customers to taste each batch before purchase, and consumers who understand and enjoy variety. This is, understandably, not something most consumers are accustomed to, being reliant on consistency-driven supermarket supply chains. Another reason these are challenging to produce is that the process of acidification caused by the lactic acid bacteria is an important part of food safety regulation and our environmental health officers do not have the same exposure to this natural method of cheesemaking, instead preferring the more consistent but less interesting process governed by standardised starter cultures.

When tasting cheeses for making notes or scoring, I do so based upon sight, smell and taste alone. However, when enjoying a cheese at the end of the day with a crusty piece of bread, I will allow knowledge of how the structure and flavours of the cheese have come into being to enhance my experience. Also, the potential for increased particularity in unpasteurised cheeses, and those created using wild cultures, is an important factor in my enjoyment. To me the joy in taste is not just about experiencing a great set of flavours but in savouring something with a narrative that speaks of its origins.

CHEESE CATEGORIES:
WHY CHEESES DIFFER

The chief method of categorising cheese is by texture, which is largely influenced by moisture content. Not every cheese readily sits within one category however, as after it has been made it may have undergone a secondary process, such as mould ripening which will also place it into a secondary category. There are cheeses that may undergo more than one secondary process, such as mould ripening as well as blue-veining, which confuses matters for anyone craving strict order. For this guide I have structured the categories into primary and, where relevant, secondary categories, and I have done so within the context of this guide, i.e. to best describe the cheeses I have included: those common to Britain and those of an artisan nature.

To better interpret the categories, a little understanding of how they come about can help.

THE MILK: COW, SHEEP, GOAT OR BUFFALO

The milk type will be a determining factor in the style of cheese made, both because of composition as well as volume produced by the animal. It is possible to make cheese from some non-ruminating animals, such as donkey or yak, but the quantity produced by ruminants has made them the primary source of milk for our cheese. Cows produce the bulk of our milk for cheese, followed by sheep and goats and then, to a lesser extent buffalo.

Milk mostly comprises water. Beyond that each type has a different nutritional composition (fats, proteins, sugars and minerals) affecting the texture and flavour of any cheese made from it. Cow's and goat's milk have similar levels of solids, approximately 12%, but sheep's milk comprises 20% and Buffalo 17%, giving them higher yields of cheese per litre of milk.

The relatively low volumes of milk given by sheep and goats, compared with cows have in some cases historically led them to be used to produce smaller cheeses. The largest types of cheese are predominantly made with cow's milk. Buffalo were not widely introduced into Britain and, as low milk yielders, they have until recently been overlooked as a significant source of cheese in this country.

Cow's milk typically produces cheeses that are sweeter and more buttery than sheep's or goat's milk and more yellow in colour, due to the presence of beta-carotene, a pigment metabolised by sheep, goats and buffalo.

With sheep's milk, the higher ratio of solids is offset by the lower volumes of milk produced per animal when compared with goats, and, whilst between the eleventh and sixteenth centuries we were a nation of sheep's milk cheese producers, they are the now the creation only of the dedicated few. At their best, sheep's milk cheeses are highly complex with aromatics associated with dried meats and nuts.

Goat's milk has smaller fat globules than cow's or sheep's, making it closer to human milk, aiding digestion, but this isn't enough to convince many to sample the cheeses from this most divisive of milk sources. The fat globules are gentler-structured and easily disrupted if poorly handled, leading to high instances of rancidity, accounting for the 'goaty' taste disliked by many. When made from the expertly handled milk of a herd fed on high quality forage, goat's milk cheeses are sweet, floral, and exhibit a range of persistent herbaceous aromatics free of any taint.

MILK TO CHEESE

Making cheese is a process of separating liquid (whey) from solid (curd). How it's done influences the style of cheese you end up with. Remove little whey and you have a softer, high moisture cheese. Remove a lot and your cheese will be harder and drier. To separate the whey from the curd, the milk needs to coagulate. This can happen over a long period due to acidification of the milk by Lactic Acid Bacteria, either naturally present or deliberately added, but happens more quickly when rennet is added.

COAGULATION

By itself, acidification produces a weak curd, which is suitable for some fresh cheeses but not for harder styles or those requiring greater ageing. So, for most cheeses, rennet is added in a quantity appropriate to the variety. Rennet contains the enzyme chymosin, a coagulant. Traditional rennet is obtained from the fourth stomach compartment (the abomasum) of calves and has been used since early in the history of cheesemaking as its effect may have been realised as soon as milk was first transported in a sack made from an abomasum. Nowadays, due to market desires, all commercial and much artisan cheese is made using vegetarian rennet, either using a coagulant derived from microbial sources or, to a lesser extent, obtained from plants such as the cardoon thistle. Many artisan producers prefer animal rennet, maintaining that its enzymes add to the complexity of aged cheeses. Indeed, some European PDO (Protected Designation of Origin) cheeses, such as Comté, stipulate the use of animal rennet.

ACIDIFICATION

Acidification occurs due to lactic acid bacteria metabolising the milk's sugar, lactose, into lactic acid. Think of them munching away to produce this precious preservative that allows us to have cheese. The acidification of milk and curd (the change continues throughout making) is an essential part of the process as it protects the cheese from undesirable bacteria. Acidification is achieved using a starter culture containing lactic acid bacteria, either purchased or cultured on-farm from the milk of the herd or flock. As mentioned above, lactic acid bacteria native to the milk would acidify it over a long period of time, but to allow nature to take its course on a day-to-day basis would be a step too far, and likely lead to alcohol or valium dependency in the cheesemaker.

HEAT AND ACTION

With coagulation now underway, how the curd sheds moisture, and the volume lost, is moderated by temperature and agitation. The higher the temperature that the curds are warmed to, the greater the moisture loss. The moistest of cheeses, fresh cheeses, will be made at temperatures as low as 20°C and the driest of hard cheeses at up to 55°C. Curd agitation (cutting and stirring) is carried out to manage the rate of moisture loss. The moistest of cheeses will be made without cutting or stirring curd prior to draining, and the driest will be cut to grain-sized pieces and stirred vigorously.

The curd for harder cheeses will have lost more moisture before they are moulded, whereas the curds for softer cheeses will lose much after draining.

MOULDING

Curds are then transferred into moulds for continued draining. The moisture to remain in the curd will largely determine the shape and size of the mould, as shape is easily lost with higher moisture, so moister cheeses tend to be made in smaller moulds. Most high moisture cheeses are unpressed or only lightly pressed, whereas the driest, hardest styles are hardest pressed to expel more whey as well as eliminate potential fissures or holes.

SALTING

To further protect from unwanted microbial activity as well as to aid flavour development, cheeses are salted. Salting can be done by direct application or via a bath of brine. With small to mid-sized cheeses salting generally takes place on the surface once the cheeses have been de-moulded. With larger cheeses, to aid even salt distribution, curds can be salted prior to moulding, as is common in British varieties, or brined.

MATURATION

Fresh cheeses are now ready for consumption. Others will require a maturation period at a constant temperature and humidity suitable for the style. The moisture content will largely determine the age of release, as higher moisture encourages greater microbial activity and thus quicker breakdown of the cheese.

AGE AT RELEASE

This guide gives an indication of the age of each cheese at release. As a rule of thumb the longer a cheese takes to age, the longer it can be kept beyond release. I think it would be fair to say, in most cases, that a cheese will comfortably last up to 50% longer than its age at release. Moreover, many cheeses will improve with a little further time to mature, as cheeses are often released prior to their prime to allow for time in transit and to extend retail shelf-life.

CHEESE CATEGORIES:
PRIMARY CATEGORIES

FRESH, UNRIPENED CHEESE

These are the simplest of cheeses, often made from goat's or sheep's milk. Young and high moisture (typically 65% or more) they are made to be consumed within days of purchase. They have no or little discernable rind and, unless aged in brine or oil, will have the shortest lifespan, as high moisture accelerates microbial activity. Due to the simple nature of their flavours, they are sometimes ash coated to increase alkalinity and thus flavour development, or rolled in another ingredient such as herbs. For this guide I have only included cheeses where the milk provides the primary aromatic source as in my opinion a dominant taste of, say, parsley little distinguishes one cheese from another, no matter how enjoyable that cheese may be. The finest fresh cheeses are every bit as capable of being of as high a quality as good aged cheese if they are made from the finest milk and in a way that amplifies the effect of the natural microflora.

SOFT CHEESE

These are cheeses with a lower moisture content than fresh cheeses and firmer at point of make, but due to microbial action will break down to form a soft inner paste. The breakdown will happen from the rind inwards due to aerobic processes happening at the rind. The breakdown is often mould-influenced, as with bloomy rind cheeses, or bacteria-influenced, as with a washed-rind, or can be due to the action of yeasts, as is common in goat's milk cheeses. Whilst the diameter of a soft cheese may be great, as in a Brie, thickness will often be limited, as if a core is too thick then the rind and under-rind would pass their best before the core were to lose its youthful chalky character. They are generally at their best at 5-10 weeks. For the cheese lover, the rind is not just a parcel for the inner goo, but an intrinsic, and some believe superior, eating experience. Brie and camembert styles fall within this category, as do many washed-rind cheeses.

SEMI SOFT CHEESE

Semi-soft cheeses generally come in larger formats than soft cheeses as their moisture is lower, allowing greater stability and a slower maturation period. They are made at higher temperatures than softer cheeses and are often lightly pressed to expel more whey and eliminate fissures. This category includes some young lightly pressed cheeses, some washed-rinded cheeses and creamy blues.

SEMI HARD CHEESE

These cheeses contain lower moisture than semi-soft cheeses and they will often be pressed. The crumbly Cheshire and Lancashire cheeses as well as more elastic Edam and young Gouda styles fall within this category. Cheddars may do too, depending on the make and age.

HARD CHEESE

These are made at higher temperatures, their curd cut the finest and they will be pressed for longer and harder than the other categories. Subsequently they are drier and capable of ageing for longer. If the milk or curd is not heated to above 40°C, they are classed as uncooked. Cheddars and most British hard traditional cheeses are uncooked. Above 40°C (up to 55°C) cheeses are classed as cooked, such as British takes on the Alpine styles like Comté or the north Italian Parmigiano-Reggiano. These cheeses are most often coated or bound in cloth, or washed and brushed to protect them during maturation.

CHEESE CATEGORIES:
SECONDARY CATEGORIES

BLOOMY RIND

These are soft cheeses whose rinds are covered in a downy white or, less often, grey mould. The white-moulds Penecillium camemberti and Penecillium candidum, or a mixture, are the most common used, often joined by Geotrichum candidum, a yeast. Types of fungi, they form a fur on the surface which serves as a protective coating as well as assisting the breakdown underneath by lowering the acidity, turning the chalky core into a creamy paste from the outside in.

WASHED RIND

Some rind washing may take place on certain hard cheeses, but a washed-rind cheese is one where the action of washing is to encourage the even development of bacteria upon the rind of a soft or semi-soft cheese. The higher moisture content allows colonies of

Brevibacterium linens and associated microflora to thrive, lowering the rind's acidity and encouraging breakdown beneath. Characterised by a tacky pink-orange surface they are the most pungent of cheeses on the nose, but the palate often has gentler characteristics. They are washed with a solution of brine, sometimes with the addition of diluted alcohol, such as ale, wine or brandy, often from a local source. The salt water discourages unwanted mould while the alcohol provides a nutrient for the bacteria.

BLUE CHEESES

Unpressed and uncooked, blue cheeses are most often semi-soft or semi-hard and gain their blue veining with the addition of Penecillium roqueforti to the milk. In semi-soft and semi-hard cheeses, the texture of the curd is made loose, allowing pockets and pathways in the cheese for the mould to inhabit. Following the make the cheeses are rubbed up to seal any fissures, thus allowing the curd's texture to alter and the curd flavours to develop before allowing the aerobic spores to germinate in the cheese. When the cheesemaker feels the time is right (which will differ from cheese to cheese and maker to maker, but typically after a few weeks), the cheeses are pierced with steel rods allowing passages of air to activate the mould. The inner surfaces of the curd in contact with the mould will respond in the same way as the surface on a bloomy rind, breaking it down to a softer consistency and imparting a richer flavour, which with Penecillium roqueforti is characterised by a spicy bite. The surfaces of some blue cheeses, such a Stilton, are mould- and bacteria-ripened too, whereas others are wrapped in foil as with Roquefort, or some even with leaves. Historically, blue cheeses would likely have been encountered as fortuitous mistakes by cheesemakers and the delicious consequence subsequently encouraged.

Arthur Alsop

ALSOP & WALKER

ALSOP & WALKER

An ambition to create a range of cheeses to fill a cheeseboard is one that few individual producers succeed in achieving. The mental resources required to master such a wide range is not far from the equivalent of becoming a baker, brewer and distiller; the key ingredient may be the same, but the techniques anything but. It's a reason many choose to specialise, particularly when attempting the business of cheesemaking for the first time.

In 2008, when Arthur Alsop set out with that ambition, he had the equipment to begin with, courtesy of a friend selling his cheesemaking business due to relocation to South Africa, but Arthur's connection to cheese was largely limited to a familiarity with livestock, but for a different purpose. The son of a beef farmer, he had spent time in his youth selling the family's cuts to the restaurants in his native Morayshire. This led to an apprenticeship as a chef, but it was his time as an entrepreneur that informed an understanding of business and marketing that underpins the Alsop & Walker enterprise today and has helped create a range of unique cheeses cannily matched to gaps in the market.

One of Alsop & Walker's first creations, Mayfield, an Alpine-Gouda cross named after the parish in which the dairy lies, Arthur had thought too niche and he had considered giving it up until a friend entered it into the British Cheese Awards. A gold was all that was needed to bring the style to the attention of chefs and restaurateurs countrywide and Mayfield now accounts for over half of the one hundred tonnes a year the dairy produces.

Soft and hard cheeses are now made in separate dairies. The former, including the iconic Lord London, a gooey cheese modelled on Galicia's Tetilla (meaning nipple, the cheese resembling a breast) are made in the original dairy at Five Ashes in the heart of rural Sussex. The hard cheeses are now made within nearby Plumpton Agricultural College's dairy, on days when Arthur isn't imparting his knowledge of how to create a cheeseboard to a new generation of cheesemakers.

WOODSIDE RED

AGE AT RELEASE

4 months

STYLE

Hard

RENNET

Vegetarian

MILK TYPE

Cow: H.F., Friesian,
Guernsey, Jersey

 6kg

  Drum

TASTING NOTE

When crumbled, the core gives aromas of toffee, pan
fried nuts and carrot cake that darken with a mineral
edge towards the rind.

WHERE TO BUY

Wholesalers and cheesemongers countrywide. See web
for details.

WHAT TO DRINK

Mid-bodied reds, semi-sweet whites, malty beer or
off-dry cider.

SUSSEX FARMHOUSE

 AGE AT RELEASE

8 months

STYLE

Hard

RENNET

Vegetarian

MILK TYPE

Cow: H.F., Friesian,
Guernsey, Jersey

 2.5kg

 Small Drum

TASTING NOTE

A richly flavoured cheese with a satisfying Cheddar
crumble yielding sweet aromatics of cereal and cashew
and a palate with a nut and wild mushroom bite.

WHERE TO BUY

Wholesalers and cheesemongers countrywide. See web
for details.

WHAT TO DRINK

Sweet whites, rich reds, malty ale, cider, whisky.

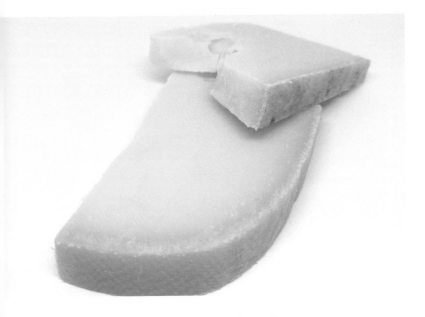

MAYFIELD

AGE AT RELEASE

6 months

STYLE

Hard

RENNET

Vegetarian

MILK TYPE

Cow: H.F., Friesian, Guernsey, Jersey

18kg

Large Drum

TASTING NOTE

A high-tone cheese with a brittle bend, giving flavours of seared chantrelle, wild flower and salted caramel on the finish. Outstanding.

WHERE TO BUY

Wholesalers and cheesemongers countrywide. See web for details.

WHAT TO DRINK

Medium to rich reds, sweet whites, tawny port, malty beer, cider.

Sarah Appleby

APPLEBY'S

:camera: @applebyscheese

:bird: @applebyscheese

:calendar: www.applebyscheese.co.uk

APPLEBY'S

Once surrounded by colleagues in cheese, the Applebys are almost alone in expressing the reason a classic came into being.

For a long time Cheshire was Britain's most popular cheese, accounting for over 50% of the entire cheese market before World War Two, but this crumbly classic lost out to Cheddar with the advent of mass-production. Cheddar's elastic solidity was better suited to bulk storage and transport. Cheddar sales now outstrip those of all other hard British territorials (cheeses named after the county or area they originated from) by ten to one. The fate of traditional Cheshire cheese has been worse than others. From over a thousand in the 1930s there are now only two artisan producers remaining and Appleby's is the only one making exclusively unpasteurised, cloth bound Cheshire.

Lucy and Lance Appleby grew up on farms, but the couple first made cheese in 1952 when they moved to Hawkstone Abbey Farm and began with Cheshire using the traditional recipe that remains little changed today. As with other producers at the time, their customer was the Milk Marketing Board, the body formed to avert the milk crisis of the 1930s and to regulate production and supply. To put it mildly, the Board's volume-led ethos was not aligned with Lucy's and she resisted change throughout. When in 1982 she came under pressure to wax coat their cheese, it was time for a change. She knew that waxing would eliminate the flavour-enhancing moulds unique to their maturation rooms so sought a new market in London and found willing buyers at Neal's Yard dairy and Paxton and Whitfield.

Second generation Edward and Christine have since passed responsibility to Paul and Sarah Appleby, who are assisted by head cheesemaker Gary Gray. They are aware of the national treasure they have inherited and the precarious task of shaping the future of a classic. They have not sought to change the recipe, instead tasking themselves to improve soil management, animal welfare and other elements that will only enhance the way the farm embodies our precious heritage.

DOUBLE GLOUCESTER

AGE AT RELEASE

14 weeks

STYLE

Hard

RENNET

Animal

MILK TYPE

Cow: Friesian,
Montbéliarde ,
Fleckvieh

8kg

Cylinder

TASTING NOTE

An outstanding cheese with crème brûlée and mushroom broth aromas and a creamy palate with flavours of caramelised vegetables, fried wild mushroom and toast. Outstanding.

WHERE TO BUY

Via website or wholesalers and cheesemongers countrywide. See web for details.

WHAT TO DRINK

Mid-bodied reds, semi-sweet whites, malty beer or off-dry cider.

CHESHIRE

AGE AT RELEASE

8 weeks

STYLE

Semi Hard

RENNET

Animal

MILK TYPE

Cow: Friesian,
Montbéliarde ,
Fleckvieh

8 KG

CYLINDER

TASTING NOTE

Beautifully crumbly with a cracked-quartz core that gives aromas of floral scented cream. Palate flavours of citrus that fade to reveal shitake mushroom and fresh herb, turning wonderfully earthy towards the rind. Outstanding.

WHERE TO BUY

Via website or wholesalers and cheesemongers countrywide. See web for details.

WHAT TO DRINK

Mid-bodied reds, semi-sweet whites, malty beer or off-dry cider.

Hugh Padfield

BATH SOFT
CHEESE COMPANY

@bathsoftcheese

@bathsoftcheese

www.parkfarm.co.uk

BATH SOFT CHEESE COMPANY

Britain's cheese heritage lies largely with the crumbly and hard territorial cheeses such as Cheshire and Cheddar, so when you spot a Bath Soft Cheese for the first time you might be forgiven for thinking that perhaps Camembert was the inspiration for Graham Padfield's bloomy-rinded creation in 1993. It was in fact a 1908 Bath grocer's recipe and a reference to 'a cream cheese of Bath manufacture' noted in a letter from Admiral Nelson's father to his son in 1801 is what spurred Graham's venture into cheesemaking.

Park Farm lies just three miles outside Bath and Graham is the third generation of the Padfields to farm a dairy herd on its rich pastures. As with all dairy farms, the pressure to scale up, sell up or diversify was looming and, not warming to the first two, Graham turned to cheesemaking. His grandmother had made Cheddar there from 1914, when she and husband Ernest bought the property, until 1939, a time when many farms gave up due to wartime restrictions. Instead of selecting the path well trodden by returning to Cheddar, Graham wanted something unique and with an unusual back-story, which he found in a Bath reference library.

The farm became certified organic in 2000, contributing to the value of any milk not processed into cheese. In the same year Wyfe of Bath, a semi-hard Gouda-inspired cheese, joined its soft sibling in the farm's canon. Bath Blue was added in 2010, followed in 2017 by Merry Wyfe, an incarnation of the Wyfe of Bath but treated with a wash of Graham's own organic cider every two days for four weeks. Now 60% of the farm's milk goes into its own cheeses, the remainder sold to premium cheese and ice cream makers.

In 2010 Graham's son Hugh, a telecommunications consultant, was lured back to the pastures he'd played in as a child and joined his father at the helm. He has reinforced the innovating habit. A new dairy, completed in 2015 with an overlooking café, is strengthening the connection between consumer and producer, a factor both see as vital for the long-term prosperity of their farm and brand, underpinned by direct sales via farmers' markets or the finer grocers of Bath.

BATH SOFT CHEESE

 AGE AT RELEASE

3 weeks

STYLE

Soft, Bloomy

RENNET

Animal

MILK TYPE

Cow: Brown Swiss, H.F.

 250g

Tile

TASTING NOTE

The delicate rind gives off shitake mushroom notes and, when cut, the gooey core gives notes of double cream, hazelnut, and white chocolate. Outstanding.

WHERE TO BUY

Via the website or wholesalers and cheesemongers countrywide. See web for details.

WHAT TO DRINK

Off-dry sparkling, aromatic white, mid-bodied fruity red.

BATH BLUE

AGE AT RELEASE

10-12 weeks

STYLE

Semi Hard, Blue

RENNET

Animal

8kg

Cylinder

TASTING NOTE

A rich and creamy core with consistent marbling, giving flavours of sauteed cashew, caramel and a delicate pepper spice. The flavour strengthens closer to the rind, turning earthy with notes of wild mushroom and hung game. Outstanding.

WHERE TO BUY

Via the website or wholesalers and cheesemongers countrywide. See web for details.

WHAT TO DRINK

Rich reds, Port, sweet whites and sweet cider.

WYFE OF BATH

AGE AT RELEASE

5 months

STYLE

Hard

RENNET

Vegetarian

MILK TYPE

Cow: Brown Swiss, H.F.

2kg

Ammonite

TASTING NOTE

Sweet vanilla and floral notes from the core richen to mineral and seared chicken breast closer to the rind.

WHERE TO BUY

Via the website or wholesalers and cheesemongers countrywide. See web for details.

WHAT TO DRINK

Medium to rich reds, sweet whites, tawny port, malty beer, cider.

MERRY WYFE

 AGE AT RELEASE

4 months

STYLE

Semi Hard, Washed-
rind

RENNET

Vegetarian

 2kg

Ammonite

TASTING NOTE

The rind gives a pungent array of sweet game, cep
mushroom and day-old sock notes (delightful for
it) and the core is gentler with creamy hazelnut and
vanilla. On the palate the rind follows in the same vein,
but the gently elastic core turns smooth with floral
notes to the fore. Outstanding.

WHERE TO BUY

Via the website or wholesalers and cheesemongers
countrywide. See web for details.

WHAT TO DRINK

Sweet whites, full-bodied reds, malty ale, ciders.

Stephen Fletcher

BERKSWELL

In 1989 the Fletcher family spotted an opportunity and took the ram by the horns. They began replacing their dairy cow herd with milking ewes and started making cheese. Their aptly named Ram Hall Farm had cheese pedigree, an upstairs room within the Elizabethan hall having once been used for cheesemaking, its floorboards etched by whey acidity.

Sheila Fletcher and neighbour Sally Rogers started with a loose-knit Caerphilly recipe, but a cheese course at Otley College in Ipswich guided Sheila towards the drier Manchego texture the cheese has today. Unlike Manchego, Berkswell is unpressed, and instead the curds are drained and turned with colanders, giving the cheese its distinctive 'flying saucer' shape. In the maturation cellar the cheese rinds develop a distinctive dry-stone wall appearance, speckled with even spots of yellow and rust-coloured moulds. The latter, Sporendonema casei, is a recent interloper found on some of the world's finest sheep's milk cheeses. To Stephen Fletcher, Sheila's son and currently at the helm, it was as welcome an addition to the dairy as any of their many awards.

Despite Britain having been almost exclusively a nation of sheep's milk cheese producers after the Norman Conquest, the style lost favour after the dissolution of the monasteries as the monks were its principal producers. Its status was further eroded by improved transport infrastructure in the eighteenth century, the higher volumes and subsequent larger cheeses permitted by milking cows making sheep a less economical source.

While sheep produce lower volumes of milk, cheese yields per litre are greater than from cows due to the higher levels of butterfats and protein. Sheep also normally 'dry off' over winter, cows being easier to calve in blocks, making a consistent supply difficult, but Stephen has developed an unusual three block milking programme, keeping this fabulous cheese in production year-round. It is a fine benchmark by which all hard sheep's milk cheese can be judged as well as affording a delicious window onto the past.

BERKSWELL

 AGE AT RELEASE

6 months

STYLE

Hard

RENNET

Animal

MILK TYPE

Sheep: Friesland

 2.3kg

Ammonite

TASTING NOTE

A satisfying spring to the core that breaks to emit aromas of dried cream on a mat of pressed flowers. The moreish palate has flavours of dried game, trompette de la mort and hay. Outstanding.

WHERE TO BUY

Wholesalers and cheesemongers countrywide.

WHAT TO DRINK

Sweet white, sherry, mid-bodied fruity red, winter ale.

Eric Horn

BIRDOSWALD

Set in spectacular frontier country on the edge of Bewcastle Fells, just north of Hadrian's Wall, Slack House Farm is holding out and prospering in the face of change.

Dairy farmers since 1978, Eric and Dianne Horn moved to the property in the late nineties and soon found the need to diversify due to low milk prices. In 2002 they began to turn a proportion of the milk from their 30 Ayrshire cows into cheese.

Named after the Roman fort overlooking the farm, Birdoswald is true to the Dunlop tradition of cheesemaking that evolved to suit the creamy milk of the Ayrshire breed, the recipe for which was brought to Dunlop in Ayrshire from Ireland by Barbara Gilmore in 1688. Barbara taught others the Dunlop method, insisting that only 'sweet' (full cream) milk could be used, as cheese in the region had hitherto only been made from milk already skimmed for its cream. Whilst like a Cheddar recipe, in that the curds are cut into blocks and stacked to assist whey removal before milling, the temperature making for Dunlop is cooler and the maturation times shorter, leading to a lighter, moister style of cheese. Birdoswald is true to type and, as an unpasteurised cheese made from a pedigree Ayrshire herd farmed organically, it is as authentic as could be.

The organic nature of their farm, whilst a bonus for their cheese (in that their 34 acres of wildflower-rich pasture impart more complex flavours), also augments the price of the milk they sell to their wholesaler, as there's now more of a premium for organic milk than when they started.

Slack House Farm is a model of resistance, but cheese is only one of the weapons Eric and Dianne deploy to ensure the survival of their smallholding in these turbulent times. A farm shop, seasonal café, accommodation and yoghurt sales all contribute to the equilibrium that would otherwise tip against them if they were reliant on milk wholesale alone.

BIRDOSWALD

AGE AT RELEASE

6 months

STYLE

Hard

RENNET

Vegetarian

MILK TYPE

Cow: Ayrshire

 9kg

Drum

TASTING NOTE

A flavoursome cheese with aromas of sweet citrus interwoven with game and an earthy palate of mixed fungi notes over a piquant chilli bite.

WHERE TO BUY

See the website for details.

WHAT TO DRINK

Rich reds, tawny port, sweet whites and sweet cider.

Tim Jarvis and Dave Holton

BLACKWOODS
CHEESE COMPANY

@blackwoodscheeseco

@blackwoodsco

www.blackwoodscheesecompany.co.uk

BLACKWOODS CHEESE COMPANY

⊙ CHIDDINGSTONE, KENT

One of London's best cheeses owes much to the Antipodes and a little to the 19th century British legal system.

A traineeship in southern Australia's Yarra Valley Dairy in 2006 began Dave Holton's career in cheese. There he learned to make a marinated fresh cheese, Persian Fetta, his penchant for which remained after his move to London in 2010. A ten-day stint as a Christmas temp at Neal's Yard Dairy became a full-time position and much of the next three years was spent refining his skills in the maturation rooms as an affineur (one who matures cheese to peak ripeness), working with some of the country's best cheesemakers to help bring their creations to the public in prime condition.

In 2013 Neal's Yard supported his move to a dairy in nearby Brockley to start his own company with two Yarra friends, Cameron Rowan and Rory Holwera. Their first cheese, Graceburn, named after a river near Dave's home town of Healesville, was a version of the original Persian Fetta, marinated in olive and rape seed oils with the addition of thyme, bay and pepper. In the same year another former Neal's Yard employee, Tim Jarvis, joined the business to head up a Blackwood's Cheese stall in Borough Market, where the cheese was given exposure to an eager footfall of experimental foodies not used to oil-marinated cheese. Tim has now largely taken over daily cheesemaking duties following the departure of Cameron and Rory.

In 2016 the company moved to where their milk is sourced, The Commonwork Organic Farm based at Bore Place near Sevenoaks in Kent, allowing them to short-circuit the passage of milk to their vats. The farm's 240 low-yielding cows produce rich milk ideal for cheesemaking which the pair now turns into a range of unpasteurised produce including fresh curd and whey.

They have launched a 'convict series' of table cheeses, named after those transported to Australia for pilfering cheese. Their signature style Edmund Tew, a Langres-influenced lactic cheese with a wrinkly washed rind, would surely put a smile on the face of its namesake, something that understandably eluded him at the time. The press then reported: 'The prisoner heard his sentence with the most perfect indifference.' This was doubtless down to the cheese he'd purloined not being up to Blackwood's lofty standards.

EDMUND TEW

AGE AT RELEASE

3 weeks

STYLE

Soft, Bloomy

RENNET

Animal

MILK TYPE

Cow: H.F.,
Montbéliarde,
Swedish Red

 150g

 Small Drum

TASTING NOTE

The rind emits delightful panoply of peanut butter in boiling cream aromas and the palate continues with notes of white chocolate. A smooth and moreish paste to the palate gives floral notes over the sweetness and a savoury white game and fried seed flavour from the core. Exceptional.

WHERE TO BUY

Wholesalers and cheesemongers in London. See web for details.

WHAT TO DRINK

Semi-sweet white, mead, malty ale.

Alex Reid

CAMBUS O'MAY

@ @cambuscheese

🐦 @cambuscheese

🗓 www.cambusomay.com

CAMBUS O'MAY

The childhood experience of a family tradition has helped give back Scotland one of its own.

A farmer's son, Alex Reid, once helped his mother make cheese on the family stove, watching as she'd add a little rennet, cut the curd and, after two or three days making, pack it all into a cast iron chessel, the traditional mould of the day. She'd then take it out to a disused railway carriage on the farm for maturation. It was for friends and family and a labour of summer as the winter was too cold for cheese ripening. Three months later they would have something to bring delight to the longer nights.

Since 2009, high in the Cairngorms among the pines and pocket lochs, Alex has been making his own version of her cheese, Cambus o'May, to that same two-day curd recipe (a throwback to the days when smallholdings could only produce enough curd for a single cheese over two or more days). The moulds are still iron, the milk still unpasteurised, the rennet still traditional, but the equipment and dairy methods, where they do not impact upon flavour, are modern. He also makes a range of Cheddar-style creations that draw their inspiration from the cheesemaking traditions and terrain of the area.

The peaks of Lochnagar, visible on a clear day, act as muses for two of the company's cheeses, all of which are named after local landmarks. Lochnagar is a three-month-old Cheddar style but made to a cooler recipe, resulting in a creamier texture. Auld Lochnagar is a twelve-month-old incarnation, bolder in flavour and drier in texture. Lairig Ghru is a moist and crumbly cheese named after a wild hill pass nearby.

Whilst the name Auld Reekie, the moniker for Edinburgh in its industrial revolution haze, is drawn from further afield, the tradition for smoked food is not. Royal Deeside is famous for its smoked salmon, game, and now, once again, cheese. The addition of smoke to cheese can sometimes be compensation for inadequate flavour, but not so with Auld Reekie, where the charred spirit flavours, imparted from the whisky barrel staves that the cheeses are smoked with, only add to the cheese's character.

Cambus o'May cheeses are fast being recognised as new Scottish classics, but Alex is only a part way on his journey, hoping to develop his own herd as the milk source and to place Cambus o'May firmly on the map with a Protected Food Name (PFN) status.

L A I R I G   G H R U

AGE AT RELEASE

8 weeks

STYLE

Hard

RENNET

Animal

MILK TYPE

Cow: Friesian, Jersey

12kg

Drum

TASTING NOTE

The moist core yields hazelnut, field mushroom and soured cream notes, richening to straw and wild mushroom at the rind.

WHERE TO BUY

Wholesalers and cheesemongers countrywide. See web for details.

WHAT TO DRINK

Aromatic off-dry whites, light reds, cider and hoppy ales.

CAMBUS O'MAY

AGE AT RELEASE

6 weeks

STYLE

Hard

RENNET

Animal

MILK TYPE

Cow: Friesian, Jersey

12.5kg

Drum

TASTING NOTE

A marbled, yielding paste with notes of grass, macadamia and sweet milk rice pudding.

WHERE TO BUY

Wholesalers and cheesemongers countrywide. See web for details.

WHAT TO DRINK

Medium to rich reds, tawny port, sweet whites, medium cider.

AULD REEKIE

AGE AT RELEASE

4 weeks

STYLE

Hard

RENNET

Animal

MILK TYPE

Cow: Friesian, Jersey

1.5kg

Drum

TASTING NOTE

A rich cheese with ripe fungus and game flavours balanced with toasty spice, caramel and spirit notes.

WHERE TO BUY

Wholesalers and cheesemongers countrywide. See web for details.

WHAT TO DRINK

Speyside whisky, rich reds, port, stout.

LOCHNAGAR

AGE AT RELEASE

3 months

STYLE

Hard

RENNET

Animal

MILK TYPE

Cow: Friesian, Jersey

12kg

Drum

TASTING NOTE

A semi strong cheese with a creamy texture and aromatics of hazelnut with a lemon bite on the palate.

WHERE TO BUY

Wholesalers and cheesemongers countrywide. See web for details.

WHAT TO DRINK

Aromatic semi-sweet whites, light chilled reds, cider and hoppy ales.

AULD LOCHNAGAR

AGE AT RELEASE

12 months

STYLE

Hard

RENNET

Animal

MILK TYPE

Cow: Friesian, Jersey

 12kg

  Drum

TASTING NOTE

A medium rich annatto-coloured Cheddar style with light dried fruit and mushroom notes.

WHERE TO BUY

Wholesalers and cheesemongers countrywide. See web for details.

WHAT TO DRINK

Sweet whites, rich reds, vintage port, malty ale, cider.

Tom Rhodes

CARRON LODGE

⊙ INGLEWHITE, LANCASHIRE

Carron Lodge's success as one of the leading wholesalers of British cheese might overshadow its origins in cheesemaking were it not for the consistency of its creations.

In 1988 Adrian Rhodes brought cheesemaking back to his family farm, a process not practised since the early 1900s. The first recipes were the farm's originals, Lancashire and Cheshire, but the range quickly expanded to make use of all the milk from their own herd in a desire to be free of punitive milk pricing. Distribution became a core part of the business, leading to the decision in 1996 to take on the cheeses of other local and then overseas producers. Rather than diminish the demand for their own cheese, this helped strengthen their own range and grow the herd. Now, among the 2000 products the company supplies, thirty are cheeses of their own making, using the milk of their 500 cows as well as goat's and sheep's milk purchased from local farms.

In 2015 a new chapter began with the acquisition of a small herd of Water Buffalo. Buffalo yield less than one fifth the milk of some cows, but the solids content is higher, resulting in rich cheeses with greater character. Shipston Blue and Inglewhite Buffalo, both matured in the farm's man-made cave alongside their other premium cheeses, have been winning awards and turning the focus back to the farm's founding pursuit.

INGLEWHITE BUFFALO

 AGE AT RELEASE
6 months

STYLE
Hard

RENNET
Vegetarian

MILK TYPE
Buffalo

2kg

Small Drum

TASTING NOTE

Dry alabaster-cracked core with rich cream pudding, vanilla and light cinnamon aromas. Dry-crumble palate feel with baked custard and almond biscuit flavours becoming darker and mineral-toned on the rind. Outstanding.

WHERE TO BUY

Wholesalers and cheesemongers countrywide. See web for details.

WHAT TO DRINK

Rich reds, port, sherry, winter ale and sweet cider.

SHIPSTON BLUE

AGE AT RELEASE

4 weeks

STYLE

Soft, Blue

RENNET

Vegetarian

MILK TYPE

Buffalo

 900g

Small Drum

TASTING NOTE

An unctuous parcel of blue-threaded goo with rich flavours of dried orchard fruit, cep and hazelnut. Outstanding.

WHERE TO BUY

Wholesalers and cheesemongers countrywide. See web for details.

WHAT TO DRINK

Medium-dry to sweet whites, tawny port, rich ale, sweet cider.

Carwyn Adams

CAWS CENARTH

One upside to the milk quota system, which between 1984 and 2015 capped the amount of milk a farmer could sell without levy, was that it turned several milk producers to cheesemaking for their surplus. In the case of Gwynfor and Thelma Adams on their farm, Glyneithinog, in the secluded wooded Cych Valley, it spurred them to revive the Welsh Caerffilli (Caerphilly) tradition.

The town of Caerphilly, like Stilton, was a market town to which makers of the eponymous cheese would come from throughout Wales as well as across the border to sell their produce. This dwindled when farmhouse production all but died out during World War II. As a looser-textured cheese with a shorter shelf life, its production was discouraged by the Milk Marketing Board. After the war, large-scale Cheddar producers revived the name, but not the nature of the cheese, seeing only the profit potential of a quick-to-market product, the reason why most today sadly associate Caerphilly with something that tastes like a cross between cheese and chalk.

In 1987, Thelma drew on six generations of family cheesemaking history and, with the assistance of pioneering cheese technologist Val Bines, she first produced a farmhouse, naturally-rinded Caerffilli now known as Thelma's Original. Thelma remains at the heart of the business but responsibility has passed to son Carwyn, who since 1999 has added depth and breadth of his own crafting. A desire to provide a complete cheese board has seen the addition of bloomy-rinded, blues, sheep's milk and washed-rind cheeses, all made to the highest levels and many multi-award winning.

GOLDEN CENARTH

 AGE AT RELEASE

5 weeks

STYLE

Soft, Washed Rind

RENNET

Vegetarian

MILK TYPE

Cow: Meuse-Rhine-Issel

200g, 1.2kg

Small Disk, Disk

TASTING NOTE

Notes of red game and earth radiate from the rind, while the palate is gentler, with field mushroom broth and double cream notes.

WHERE TO BUY

Farm shop, via website or wholesalers and cheesemongers countrywide. See web for details.

WHAT TO DRINK

Semi-sweet white, mead, malty ale.

CAWS CENARTH BRIE

 AGE AT RELEASE

3 weeks

STYLE

Soft, Bloomy

RENNET

Vegetarian

MILK TYPE

Cow: Meuse-Rhine-Issel

200g, 1.2kg

Small Disk, Disk

TASTING NOTE

A well-crafted take on the style with pearlescent rind over tawny ridges. Classic sauerkraut aromas join pigeon breast and elegant herbal notes on a palate. Outstanding.

WHERE TO BUY

Farm shop, via website or wholesalers and cheesemongers countrywide. See web for details.

WHAT TO DRINK

Sparkling, aromatic whites, light reds, hoppy ale and cider.

PERL WEN

AGE AT RELEASE

4 weeks

STYLE

Soft, Bloomy

RENNET

Vegetarian

MILK TYPE

Cow: Meuse-Rhine-Issel

Small Disk, Disk

TASTING NOTE

Highly characterful, with aromas reminiscent of fresh mushroom, chestnut and crème Chantilly. Outstanding.

WHERE TO BUY

Farm shop, via website or wholesalers and cheesemongers countrywide. See web for details.

WHAT TO DRINK

Sparkling, aromatic whites, light reds, hoppy ale and cider.

PERL LAS

 AGE AT RELEASE

2 months

STYLE

Semi Soft, Blue

RENNET

Vegetarian

MILK TYPE

Cow: Meuse-Rhine-
Issel

 400g, 2.6kg

 Small Disk, Disk

TASTING NOTE

The rich creamy core bestows a heady scent of sweet
cream, morels and orchard fruit, and the even blueing
adds a piquant fungus nip to the palate.

WHERE TO BUY

Farm shop, via website or wholesalers and
cheesemongers countrywide. See web for details.

WHAT TO DRINK

Sweet whites, tawny port, medium cider.

CENARTH CAERFFILI

AGE AT RELEASE

4 weeks

STYLE

Semi Hard

RENNET

Vegetarian

MILK TYPE

Cow: Meuse-Rhine-Issel

1.5kg

Drum

TASTING NOTE

Clean, lactic and gently saline with a pleasing crumble.

WHERE TO BUY

Farm shop, via website or wholesalers and cheesemongers countrywide. See web for details.

WHAT TO DRINK

Aromatic off-dry whites, light chilled reds, cider and hoppy ales.

THELMA CAERFFILI

AGE AT RELEASE

8 weeks

STYLE

Semi Hard

RENNET

Vegetarian

MILK TYPE

Cow: Meuse-Rhine-Issel

2.6kg

Drum

TASTING NOTE

Richer and nuttier than the Cenarth Caerffili, with dried fruit and hazelnut notes on the core, strengthening at the rind to earthy game and field mushroom. Outstanding.

WHERE TO BUY

Farm shop, via website or wholesalers and cheesemongers countrywide. See web for details.

WHAT TO DRINK

Aromatic off-dry whites, medium-bodied reds, cider and hoppy ales.

John Savage-Onstwedder

CAWS TEIFI

◎ @cawsteifi

▢ www.teificheese.co.uk

CAWS TEIFI

In 1982, at a time when there was only a handful of artisan cheesemakers left making raw milk cheeses in the UK, John and Patrice Savage-Onstwedder arrived in Wales from their native Netherlands and brought Gouda-making to the rolling hills of Ceredigion.

From a background in sustainable and organic farming, John's primary concerns were that their business should respect everything it impacted and that their cheese reflect the environment. To this end their cheeses are unpasteurised as John's views on pasteurisation are uncompromising, believing it an unnatural practice that destroys natural microflora beneficial to health, and eliminates any potential for the aromatic properties they bring. The most important business partner they work with is their milk producer. Caws Teifi has a long-standing relationship with a local small farm, from whom they take most of the milk, and at a premium recognising the nature of the artisan produce it goes to create. This relationship allows John a say in gearing the milk towards his needs and helps re-investment in the dairy farm and its small, quality-focused herd.

John began with what is now known as Teifi Natural, a classic Gouda-style cheese. The recipe for Gouda differs from other hard cheeses in that the curds are 'washed' by removing a proportion of the whey and replacing it with hot water, removing some of the lactose that gives a tang to cheeses like Cheddar, thus making gouda styles sweeter and nuttier in texture. Ever questing, John expanded their Gouda range to include nettle, cumin, and onion & garlic Teifi amongst others. The addition of herbs and spices to cheese can be a way of introducing flavour to bland cheese, but at Caws Teifi there is no compromise on the base cheese's quality and the additions are grounded in centuries-old Dutch tradition.

In the nineties the couple employed Cyril Wooley, a Caerphilly specialist, as cheesemaker. It was a move that led to the joint creation with James Aldridge (a leading figure in the revival of raw milk cheese) of Celtic Promise, a washed-rind Caerphilly which has become a staple for Caws Teifi and one of the UK's most highly awarded cheeses. Whichever cheese you choose, you will be assured of an authentic taste of this verdant part of Wales.

CAWS TEIFI

AGE AT RELEASE

3 months to 3 years

STYLE

Hard

RENNET

Animal

MILK TYPE

Cow: Holstein Friesian

8kg, 16kg

Drum

TASTING NOTE

Even, small-holed core yielding toffee apple, cashew and butter notes. A palate full of savoury grain, marmite and mixed nut flavours. Outstanding.

WHERE TO BUY

Farm shop, via website or wholesalers and cheesemongers countrywide. See web for details.

WHAT TO DRINK

Off-dry whites, full-bodied reds, malty ale, ciders.

CELTIC PROMISE

 AGE AT RELEASE

10 weeks

STYLE

Hard

RENNET

Animal

MILK TYPE

Cow: Holstein
Friesian

500g

Drum

TASTING NOTE

Lovely, even-coloured rind with a nose of warm game. Mid
depth on the palate, creamy and appealing with Brazil nut,
pigeon breast and hay flavours. Outstanding.

WHERE TO BUY

Farm shop, via website or wholesalers and cheesemongers
countrywide. See web for details.

WHAT TO DRINK

Off-dry whites, full-bodied reds, malty ale, ciders.

SAVAL

AGE AT RELEASE

10 weeks

STYLE

Semi Hard, Washed
Rind

RENNET

Animal

MILK TYPE

Cow: Holstein
Friesian

 2kg

 Drum

TASTING NOTE

The thin rind gives way to a semi-elastic core with small, even
bubbles. Sweet caramel notes over fresh herb and peanut on the
nose, and on the palate a super-giving structure with flavours
of clotted cream, chanterelle, fried pigeon breast and earth.

WHERE TO BUY

Farm shop, via website or wholesalers and cheesemongers
countrywide. See web for details.

WHAT TO DRINK

Semi-sweet whites, rich reds, malty ale and off-dry cider.

CHARLES MARTELL
& SON

⊙ DYMOCK, GLOUCESTERSHIRE

Polymath pioneer Charles Martell has many credits to his name but the one that concerns him least is the fame accrued by his Stinking Bishop Cheese when it appeared in the film 'Wallace and Gromit: The Curse of the Were-Rabbit' in 2005. It propelled the cheese to national consciousness, a factor that the company could have cashed in on, but Stinking Bishop remains firmly artisan and as good as the day it was created in 1994. The cheese, a pungent perry-washed type, takes its name from a variety of pear grown on the farm, which in turn was named after Frederick Bishop, a 19th century local farmer known for his bawdy behaviour.

The story at Charles Martell's Hunts Court farm began in 1972 when he began hand milking three Gloucester cows, a breed then close to extinction, to make a Double Gloucester cheese. Six years later he revived the Single Gloucester tradition, a cheese that hadn't been made since the 1950s, and he went on to champion the development of the PDO (Protected designation of Origin) for the style, awarded in 2007. The PDO requires the inclusion of milk from Gloucester cows, a factor helping to maintain the breed.

Whilst much of the milk is now bought locally for the cheese range, which now numbers seven, a herd of Gloucester cows still grazes the 30 acres of pastures and orchards at Hunts Court. The orchards contain some of the 100 varieties of apple and 100 varieties of pear that Charles has assiduously documented and grafted over time, their preservation a passion for him as strong as that for his cows.

At first glance, the scene at Hunt's Farm is one more redolent of Normandy, a comparison reinforced by the building of a distillery in 2010, but a look at the deeds reveals a resurrection of the distilling tradition, as the building had been used to the same ends in the 1700s.

The farm is in its essence a cornerstone of Gloucestershire tradition and one that can serve as a model for anyone wishing to stimulate interest in our rich gastronomic past.

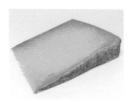

DOUBLE GLOUCESTER

 AGE AT RELEASE

2 months

STYLE

Hard

RENNET

Animal

MILK TYPE

Cow: Gloucester, Friesian

 2.2kg

 Drum

TASTING NOTE

The core gives a bowl of mixed nuts with walnut and Brazils to the fore, backed by gentle caramel notes. The core palate has a nice yielding bounce before reaching a fine grain paste with brothy red meat notes laced with dried herbs. Outstanding.

WHERE TO BUY

Wholesalers and cheesemongers countrywide. See website.

WHAT TO DRINK

Mid-bodied reds, semi-sweet whites, malty beer or off-dry cider.

STINKING BISHOP

 AGE AT RELEASE

4 weeks

STYLE

Soft, Washed Rind

RENNET

Vegetarian

MILK TYPE

Cow: Gloucester, Friesian

 1.8kg, 500g

 Disk

TASTING NOTE

A lovely wet-leather rind covers a consistent paste emitting pleasing fried honey and almond notes on the nose over the tradmark sweet-sock smell. A slippery viscosity on the palate releases rich cashew, sweetened cream and light game flavours turning musky at the rind. Outstanding.

WHERE TO BUY

Via website or wholesalers and cheesemongers countrywide. See web for details.

WHAT TO DRINK

Aromatic off-dry white, light red, medium cider or malty ale.

Jane Bowyer

CHEESEMAKERS
OF CANTERBURY

@cheesesofkent

www.cheesemakersofcanterbury.co.uk

CHEESEMAKERS
OF CANTERBURY

Jane Bowyer and Cheesemakers of Canterbury are synonymous with Kentish food heritage whose reach goes well beyond their county boundaries.

Until 2006 Jane had been running Dargate Dairy, a small supplier of milk, cream and yoghurt to locals, but industry consolidation and price pressure from supermarkets forced its sale to a national company. Jane resolved to continue providing her customers with a high-quality product from local milk, rather than see it processed for the bulk market, so she changed tack, bought a cheese recipe and equipment from retiring Wiltshire cheesemakers David and Pat Doble, and partnered with one of the dairy's farms.

The Dobles had developed a good following for Ashmore, their Cheddar recipe cheese. The temptation for Jane could have been to make the most of the name and look to where savings might be made, but instead she continued to produce Ashmore as a handmade, unpasteurised, hand-pressed, naturally-rinded cheese that required turning and brushing daily (the latter to avoid cheese mite and ensure even distribution of mould spores).

Jane's Kent customer base was ready for her new product and the business grew quickly. As well as a passion for cheesemaking she has since built up a dedicated team of cheesemakers who have helped the business develop a range of eighteen cheeses, including Ashmore-recipe goat's and sheep's milk cheeses, as well as soft bloomy-rinds and butter. Jane still buys all her cow's milk from Debden Farm in Petham, at a cheesemaking rate that allows the farm to maintain their small cheese-focused herd and produce low volumes of rich milk whose quality shines through in Ashmore. A second dairy has been established in Hastingleigh, near

Ashford, to produce pasteurised soft cheeses, and Jane has a permanent shop in the Goods Shed, Canterbury's innovative local food market.

Proximity to the Channel Tunnel helped find an enthusiastic market in France. Less a case of coals to Newcastle with Ashmore, more a novel style introduced to a demanding and appreciative cheese nation.

ASHMORE

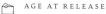

AGE AT RELEASE
6 months

STYLE
Hard

RENNET
Vegetarian

MILK TYPE
Cow: Friesian

2kg, 4kg

Drum

TASTING NOTE
A creamy Cheddar with sweet nut and spun sugar nose and a palate of cream of mushroom, Brazil nut and a citric kick.

WHERE TO BUY
Wholesalers and cheesemongers countrywide. See web for details.

WHAT TO DRINK
Off-dry whites, medium to rich reds, tawny port, malty ale, cider.

ANCIENT ASHMORE

AGE AT RELEASE

12 months

STYLE

Hard

RENNET

Vegetarian

MILK TYPE

Cow: Friesian

2kg, 4kg

Drum

TASTING NOTE

A dry, hard crumble to the core with a leather rind. Strong game notes on the core are joined by dried apple and citrus. The rind gives deep earthy flavours with notes of bark, ground seed, and nut. Outstanding.

WHERE TO BUY

Wholesalers and cheesemongers countrywide. See web for details.

WHAT TO DRINK

Sweet whites, rich reds, tawny port, malty ale, cider.

ASHMORE TOP SHELF

AGE AT RELEASE

18 months

STYLE

Hard

RENNET

Vegetarian

MILK TYPE

Cow: Friesian

 2kg, 4kg

 Drum

TASTING NOTE

Still drier than Ancient. The core emits scents of dessicated apple, beeswax, and Brazil nut and the palate follows through with a crunchy mouthful of wild boar prosciutto, cigar leaf and oak, with pleasing moodier characters towards the rind. Outstanding.

WHERE TO BUY

Wholesalers and cheesemongers countrywide. See web for details.

WHAT TO DRINK

Sweet whites, rich reds, vintage port, malty ale, cider.

Billy Kevan

COLSTON BASSETT

@colstonbassettdairy

@colstonbassett

www.colstonbassettdairy.co.uk

COLSTON BASSETT

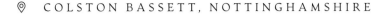

Colston Bassett Dairy has become a cornerstone of British artisan cheese production, creating a benchmark product as famed for its consistency as for its quality.

For the dairy consistency has in part been achieved through consolidation. The four farms of low-output herds supplying milk to the dairy are an amalgamation of the original sixteen that Dr William Windley helped bring together in 1912 when he founded the dairy. The farms, all of which are shareholders, lie within one and a half miles of the dairy, which occupies a half acre of land Dr Windley purchased from a squire on an isolated crossroads outside of the village.

Consistency in the one type of cheese has led to refinement of a style. Apart from two breaks for the World Wars, the focus has been solely upon Stilton and latterly its colourful but oddly-named sister, Shropshire blue. Oddly named, as Shropshire blue is predominantly orange and was first made by a Stilton-trained cheesemaker in Inverness. Like Stilton but matured for a shorter period, it has a gentler character, the annatto colouring serving to distinguish the cheeses rather than influence flavour. There had, until recently, never been any Shropshire Blue made in the county of Shropshire.

Consistency extends to the people too, with only four cheesemakers at the helm at Colston Bassett since its inception. The latest, Billy Kevan, has helped take the dairy to new heights with a rare level of meticulous oversight, as demonstrated by the regiments of Stiltons sitting on their pine beds as an orderly progression from pale cream when fresh to snow-dusted russet when ready for release.

SHROPSHIRE BLUE

AGE AT RELEASE

6 weeks

STYLE

Semi Hard, Blue

RENNET

Animal

MILK TYPE

Cow: Friesian,
Holstein Fresian,
Ayrshire

8kg

Cylinder

TASTING NOTE

The semi-strong rind emits muted wild mushroom notes lying beneath the scent of caramel and rice pudding. The theme at the core is twofold, with the blue vein's piquant spice complementing the saline cream character of the paste. Outstanding.

WHERE TO BUY

Farm shop or wholesalers and cheesemongers countrywide. See web for details.

WHAT TO DRINK

Rich reds, port, sweet whites and medium cider.

STILTON

 AGE AT RELEASE

8 weeks

STYLE

Semi Hard, Blue

RENNET

Animal

MILK TYPE

Cow: Friesian,
Holstein Fresian,
Ayrshire

 8kg

 Cylinder

TASTING NOTE

A virtual walk down a breakfast buffet: sweetened cream, cereal and cashew aromas mingle with those of dried apple and apricot. On the palate, the cheese is a masterclass in balancing blue-veined Christmas spices with sweet curd flavours. Exceptional.

WHERE TO BUY

Farm shop or wholesalers and cheesemongers countrywide. See web for details.

WHAT TO DRINK

Rich reds, port, sweet whites and medium cider.

Jill Clarke

CONNAGE HIGHLAND DAIRY

@connagecheese

@connagecheese

www.connage.co.uk

CONNAGE HIGHAND DAIRY

In the early nineties Jill Clark swapped Western Australia's outback for the Highlands. After working as a jilleroo on her parent's million-acre cattle station, she moved to the pastures of Inverness where she met husband Callum Clarke.

The Clark family had been producing milk from the clover-rich fields abutting the Moray Firth since the 1950s, when Jill's father-in-law, Hamish, moved there from Turiff in Aberdeenshire. He and his wife started a small dairy herd that sons Callum and Cameron took over in the late nineties. Seeking the added value necessitated for all UK dairy farms, both then and now, they sought to diversify rather than simply scale up.

There was little organic milk available locally, so they decided to benefit from the premiums it attracted and went about converting their practices. The farm was certified organic in 2002, however the punishingly low milk prices at the time meant that still more was needed for the farm to sustain the two families. In 2006, after training and trials, Jill and Callum began making cheese. They started with Cheddar and soon after came Dunlop, the moister version of Cheddar native to Scotland. A desire to appeal to different tastes has led them to a Brie style, goudas and smoked versions of their other cheeses. The range has helped them provide for a local demand that values provenance.

Crowdies, the traditional Scottish fresh cheese, both naked and flavoured, are also popular choices at the dairy's cheese cave and café, both essential initiatives in the Clark's recipe for success. Retail is responsible for 25% of the sales of their cheeses, without which balancing the books would be trickier.

Their pastures' salt-sprayed grasses and diverse herbage, for which moisture is rarely a problem, impart their cheeses with a flavour not to be drawn from sun-cracked outback soil, providing some compensation for the dramatic climate swap.

CLAVA

AGE AT RELEASE

3 weeks

STYLE

Soft, Bloomy

RENNET

Vegetarian

MILK TYPE

Cow: Jersey, Holstein Friesian, Norweigan Red

250g, 1.5kg

Small Disk, Disk

TASTING NOTE

Pleasant vegetal Camembert nose with notes of braised cabbage, herbs and fresh mushroom. On the palate, creamy and clean with hay and lemony hints.

WHERE TO BUY

Via the website or wholesalers and cheesemongers countrywide. See web for details.

WHAT TO DRINK

Sparkling, chilled light red, dry white, cider.

GOUDA

AGE AT RELEASE

3 months

STYLE

Hard

RENNET

Vegetarian

MILK TYPE

Cow: Jersey, Holstein
Friesian, Norweigan
Red

 14kg

 Drum

TASTING NOTE

Pistachio, toffee-brittle and toast aromas on the nose
and a sweet, semi-elastic palate of butter-fried pear,
brown sugar and hay flavours. Outstanding.

WHERE TO BUY

Via the website or wholesalers and cheesemongers
countrywide. See web for details.

WHAT TO DRINK

Sweet whites, rich reds, tawny port, malty ale, strong
cider.

DUNLOP

 AGE AT RELEASE

5 months

STYLE

Hard

RENNET

Vegetarian

MILK TYPE

Cow: Jersey, Holstein
Friesian, Norweigan
Red

 25kg

 Large Drum

TASTING NOTE

A soft-textured cheese with flavours of fresh hay and
nut.

WHERE TO BUY

Via the website or wholesalers and cheesemongers
countrywide. See web for details.

WHAT TO DRINK

Aromatic off-dry whites, light chilled reds, cider and
hoppy ales.

CHEDDAR

 AGE AT RELEASE

18 months

STYLE

Hard

RENNET

Vegetarian

MILK TYPE

Cow: Jersey, Holstein
Friesian, Norweigan
Red

 25kg

 Large Drum

TASTING NOTE

A robust Cheddar with clean notes of sweet cream,
walnut and singed hay with a gentle bite on the finish.

WHERE TO BUY

Via the website or wholesalers and cheesemongers
countrywide. See web for details.

WHAT TO DRINK

Sweet whites, rich reds, vintage port, malty ale, cider.

Mary and Ross Davenport

COTE HILL CHEESE

@cotehillcheese

@cotehillcheese

www.cotehill.com

COTE HILL CHEESE

The strikingly vibrant range at Cote Hill Cheese came about when Michael and Mary Davenport found they were losing money during the period of low milk prices in the early 2000s.

They realised that their small herd would become increasingly unsustainable unless they were to generate a greater income from the relatively low yields. Unwilling to scale up or push the cows harder, Michael took a course in cheesemaking at Reaseheath College in Cheshire. There, lecturer Chris Ashby guided them towards their first cheese, Cote Hill Blue.

To attempt a blue cheese in a county that borders those responsible for Stilton might seem like marketing folly, but they chose a soft, brie-like blue. For many this might have been cheesemaking madness, as to create the veining in a blue before the core becomes molten is notoriously tricky, yet it was this deterrent that persuaded the couple to press ahead.

Cote Hill Blue was a considerable success and has found a wide following, but as with many a farmer-turned-cheesemaker, this was no get-rich-quick scheme, more a labour of love borne out of a desire to remain in farming, continuing to practice what they were good at, while adding new skills for profit. Mary quickly found she had a passion that helped mitigate the long hours, one that has found its way to the next generation. Son Joe joined Mary in the make room in 2011 and is now responsible for new cheeses he had a hand in developing. Ross joined his father managing the cows in 2015, thus completing an unplanned succession for a small dairy farm, something as rare as blue vein brie.

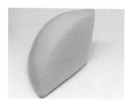

COTE HILL YELLOW

AGE AT RELEASE

6 Weeks

STYLE

Semi Hard

RENNET

Vegetarian

MILK TYPE

Cow: Friesian,
Holstein, Red Poll

1.4kg

Dome

TASTING NOTE

A pleasant, even core, with clean buttery flavours.

WHERE TO BUY

Via website or wholesalers and cheesemongers countrywide.
See web for details.

WHAT TO DRINK

Aromatic off-dry whites, light chilled reds, cider and hoppy ales.

COTE HILL RED

AGE AT RELEASE

4 months

STYLE

Hard

RENNET

Vegetarian

MILK TYPE

Cow: Friesian,
Holstein, Red Poll

4kg

Drum

TASTING NOTE

Ripe cream and straw notes from an even, fine-grain core.

WHERE TO BUY

Via website or wholesalers and cheesemongers countrywide.
See web for details.

WHAT TO DRINK

Sweet whites, rich reds, tawny port, malty ale, strong cider.

COTE HILL LINDUM

AGE AT RELEASE

8 Weeks

STYLE

Semi Hard, Washed Rind

RENNET

Animal

MILK TYPE

Cow: Friesian, Holstein, Red Poll

1.6kg

Drum

TASTING NOTE

A washed rind with a fine grain core giving pleasing game and dried mushroom notes.

WHERE TO BUY

Via website or wholesalers and cheesemongers countrywide. See web for details.

WHAT TO DRINK

Aromatic off-dry whites, light chilled reds, cider and hoppy ales.

COTE HILL BLUE

AGE AT RELEASE

8 Weeks

STYLE

Soft, Blue

RENNET

Vegetarian

MILK TYPE

Cow: Friesian, Holstein, Red Poll

1.2kg, 320g

Disk

TASTING NOTE

Multi-layered in texture and flavour, this creamy blue has a fine balance between salted cream and field mushroom with a lingering blue bite.

WHERE TO BUY

Via website or wholesalers and cheesemongers countrywide. See web for details.

WHAT TO DRINK

Sweet whites, tawny port, medium cider.

Robin Skailes

CROPWELL BISHOP
CREAMERY

 @cropwellbishopcreamery

 @yummystilton

 www.cropwellbishopstilton.co.uk

CROPWELL BISHOP CREAMERY

The third largest of Stilton's six dairies, Cropwell Bishop accounts for around 12% of this PDO (Protected Designation of Origin) and trademark certified cheese. Run by cousins Robin and Ben Skailes, the 100-year old dairy was purchased by their grandfather in 1949 but during rationing at the time Stilton was banned as the dairy, along with many others, was required to concentrate on government-permitted styles such as Cheddar and Red Leicester. Though Stilton production returned at the dairy with the end of rationing, Cropwell Bishop continued with a diverse range until the 1980's when Robin and Ben's fathers decided to specialise in this staple of the Vale of Belvoir.

Stilton can only be produced in the counties of Nottinghamshire, Leicestershire and Derbyshire and not in the Cambridgeshire town of Stilton itself, which was the cheese's marketing point, being situated on the Great North Road. It must also be made from pasteurised milk. At Cropwell Bishop the cheese is pasteurised on arrival, after which it receives its starter and Penicillium roqueforti cultures, then the rennet. The curd is cut a couple of hours later and hand-ladled onto a draining table where it is left to settle overnight. This helps create the correct consistency to develop the blue veining, air pockets in the resulting cheese being imperative. The curd is then filled into hoops and matured for a couple of days before the rind is 'sealed' by rubbing it with a palette knife. At around five weeks the cheeses are pierced, allowing air to the penicillin spores and encouraging development of the blue mould.

The dairy now processes the milk of mostly British Friesians from fourteen local farms into over 150,000 Stiltons a year. Drawing on their blue cheese heritage, Robin has added Beauvale to the range, a Gorgonzola-inspired creamy blue that in the few years since its inception has become a British classic.

BEAUVALE

 AGE AT RELEASE

8 weeks

STYLE

Semi Soft, Blue

RENNET

Animal

MILK TYPE

Cow: Friesian,
Montbéliarde , Jersey

 7kg

 Cylinder

TASTING NOTE

A characterful cheese offering a balance between gently salted cream notes over fresh mushroom, with a pepper finish from the mid-piquant blue veining.

WHERE TO BUY

Via website or wholesalers and cheesemongers countrywide. See web for details.

WHAT TO DRINK

Sweet whites, tawny port, medium cider.

STILTON

 AGE AT RELEASE

12 weeks

STYLE

Semi Hard, Blue

RENNET

Vegetarian

MILK TYPE

Cow: Friesian,
Montbéliarde , Jersey

 8kg

 Cylinder

TASTING NOTE

Lovely marbling throughout giving mixed spice notes
leading to a creamy palate of chanterelle mushroom,
dried orchard fruit and white game. Earthier towards
the rind, a forest floor. Not to be missed.

WHERE TO BUY

Via website or wholesalers and cheesemongers
countrywide. See web for details.

WHAT TO DRINK

Rich reds, port, sweet whites and medium cider.

Peter Kindel

DAYLESFORD

◎   KINGHAM, GLOUCESTERSHIRE

Powered by JCB, Daylesford Farm has become a beacon for anyone wishing better to understand sustainability as well as diversity in farming. A pioneer at a time when organic was considered quirky, Carole Bamford, wife of the engineering company's CEO, converted the family farm at Daylesford to organic practices in 1974, her impetus then solely to provide her family better food.

She has since grown the business, pursuing a policy towards maximum sustainability through enlightened soil management, renewable energy sources, high animal welfare and care for wildlife habitat. The Daylesford Farm shop is the conduit, along with sister shops in London, by which much of the farm's produce reaches the consumer. Whilst it can only have helped to have the backing of a multinational, the policy of creating high welfare food and selling it directly to the consumer is one that works financially too, retaining profits normally made by wholesaler and retailer and reinvesting them on the farm.

Amongst its output Daylesford produces meat, poultry, vegetables, salads and baked goods, so you might think cheese could easily get sidelined. Not with far-sighted head cheesemaker Peter Kindel at the helm. Peter, a New Yorker, started making cheese at home in the early nineties while working as a chef. The lure of curdling milk was strong and prompted his travels to France, followed by a cheesemaking scholarship.

He made cheese across the US before answering an advert for his current position in 2012. Since then Peter has built on the passions of previous head cheesemakers to develop and expand the wide range of world-class cheeses from the farm's well nurtured cows. These include the rare breed Gloucester cattle, the milk from which is reserved for their Single and Double Gloucester cheeses. Single

Gloucester is covered by a Protected Designation of Origin (PDO) stipulating the use of at least a little Gloucester cattle milk, a move that has helped preserve the breed, but Daylesford is unusual in using it exclusively for all their Gloucester cheeses.

DAYLESFORD BLUE

 AGE AT RELEASE

8 weeks

STYLE

Semi Soft, Blue

RENNET

Vegetarian

MILK TYPE

Cow: Friesian, Gloucester

 1.5kg

 Drum

TASTING NOTE

Clean, well made and balanced, presenting a crème Chantilly nose and macadamia nut flavour threaded with veins of warm-spice blue. Integrated and lasting.

WHERE TO BUY

Farm shop, via website or wholesalers and cheesemongers countrywide. See web for details.

WHAT TO DRINK

Tawny or vintage port, sweet whites and dessert gin.

SINGLE GLOUCESTER

AGE AT RELEASE
4 weeks

STYLE
Hard

RENNET
Animal

MILK TYPE
Cow: Gloucester

3.5kg

Drum

TASTING NOTE
A serious and masterful mouthful of warm cream laced with flavours of fresh hay, hazelnut, horse mushrooms and dried orchard fruit. Outstanding.

WHERE TO BUY
Farm shop, via website or wholesalers and cheesemongers countrywide. See web for details.

WHAT TO DRINK
Aromatic off-dry whites, light chilled reds, cider and hoppy ales.

DOUBLE GLOUCESTER

AGE AT RELEASE
8 weeks

STYLE
Hard

RENNET
Animal

MILK TYPE
Cow: Gloucester

3.5kg

Drum

TASTING NOTE
Hints of caramel on the palate lift baked apple, chanterelle and mineral flavours. Outstanding.

WHERE TO BUY
Farm shop, via website or wholesalers and cheesemongers countrywide. See web for details.

WHAT TO DRINK
Mid-bodied reds, semi-sweet whites, malty beer or off-dry cider.

Neill, James and Maggie Maxwel

DODDINGTON

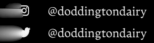 @doddingtondairy

@doddingtondairy

www.doddingtoncheese.co.uk

DODDINGTON

Nestled in the sparsely-populated 'Dark Skies' country at the eastern edge of the Cheviot Hills, Doddington Dairy is a shining beacon of hope for the small-scale dairy farmer.

Malcolm Maxwell, son of a generations-old farming tradition, moved his herd to the Glendale Valley in 1950, seeking a climate drier and sunnier than his native Dumfriesshire. Despite not being a dairy region, the move was a good one and the farm a success, but over time the dual pressures of the quota system and milk pricing coupled with the farm's remoteness meant that diversification was inevitable.

In 1992 his children, Neill and Maggie, set out to create cheese, and after cheesemaking courses at Reaseheath and Brackenhurst colleges, as well as travel to France and Holland, they set about converting some of the stone-walled barns into dairy and maturation rooms akin to the Ayrshire cheese loft their grandmother talked of once having.

Their first creation, Doddington, a Leicester-Cheddar hybrid, is a 'cool-scalded' recipe (the curd heated in the vat to 36°C, less than for Cheddar) with a nod to Gouda. Other cheeses have followed, all regionally titled: Berwick Edge, a rich Gouda style named after the range abutting the valley; Admiral Collingwood, a Newcastle Brown Ale washed-rind named in homage to the Geordie lad who became an associate of Lord Nelson; and Cuddy's Cave, a mellow, Dales-inspired cheese named after a sandstone cave on the Northumberland coast where St Cuthbert's body was said to have been laid to rest by the Lindisfarne monks.

They were soon selling to a nearby ice cream and milk parlour, which in 2000 acted as inspiration for Neill and his wife, Jackie, to branch out into ice cream, Maggie then taking the lead with cheesemaking. James, Maggie's nephew, has taken on cheese duties too and helped develop Darling Blue, named after Grace Darling, the Bamburgh lighthouse keeper's daughter who in 1838 rowed shipwreck survivors ashore in seas too rough for a lifeboat. Neill is still responsible for the farming, along with brothers Bob and John, and other family members are among the operation's twenty-strong team, a factor at the heart of what they do and a chief reason for their success.

To be successful over time, you must also be uniquely different and appealing to stand out, and with their family-crafted recipes it's a resilient combination that should the see the creations at Doddington casting a bright glow in Dark Skies country for many years to come.

ADMIRAL COLLINGWOOD

 AGE AT RELEASE

8 months

STYLE

Semi Hard, Washed Rind

RENNET

Animal

MILK TYPE

Cow: Ayrshire, Fresian, Montbéliarde

 1.5kg

 Drum

TASTING NOTE

Peanut brittle notes on the nose and a semi-elastic palate full of rich characters: fried pigeon, cep and toast notes, turning to peanuts at the rind. Outstanding.

WHERE TO BUY

Via the website or wholesalers and cheesemongers countrywide. See web for details.

WHAT TO DRINK

Semi-sweet sparkling, rich whites, medium-bodied reds, rich beer, cider.

DODDINGTON

AGE AT RELEASE

12 months

STYLE

Hard

RENNET

Animal

MILK TYPE

Cow: Ayrshire,
Fresian, Montbéliarde

 5kg

Drum

TASTING NOTE

Characterful cheese with a hard crumble, giving sweet Brazil nut, light dried meat and apple notes on the nose and a rich palate of creamy seed, hay and almond cake.

WHERE TO BUY

Via the website or wholesalers and cheesemongers countrywide. See web for details.

WHAT TO DRINK

Medium-bodied reds, sweet whites, malty beer, cider.

BERWICK EDGE

AGE AT RELEASE

12 months

STYLE

Hard

RENNET

Animal

MILK TYPE

Cow: Ayrshire,
Fresian, Montbéliarde

 5kg

Drum

TASTING NOTE

A medium sweet nose of mixed grain and hay leads to a palate with an upfront bite yielding to hazelnut and dried mushroom notes.

WHERE TO BUY

Via the website or wholesalers and cheesemongers countrywide. See web for details.

WHAT TO DRINK

Rich reds, sweet whites, malty beer, cider.

Ann Doward

DUNLOP DAIRY

DUNLOP DAIRY

———————

There are few cheesemakers as industrious as Ann Doward of The Dunlop Dairy. It's often said that if you do what you love, you'll never work a day in your life. If you tend cows and goats, milk them yourself, make cheese three times a week, run a café and keep horses on a smallholding, then you'd better be doing what you love.

A childhood passion for animals guided Ann to study agriculture. In 1983 the family moved to Clerkland Farm, a smallholding in the hills outside Dunlop. This was at a time when farming was scaling up to maintain viability and Ann knew that she would eventually have to add value to generate revenue from its small acreage.

She hit on the idea of cheesemaking and began building a herd of goats and a flock of sheep and renovating the old farm buildings, all whilst working at a local dairy farm. In 1989 she made her first cheeses, which were met with local acclaim. She soon added cow's milk to her repertoire, selecting Ayrshire cows as the obvious choice.

Once known as the Dunlop cow, the Ayrshire is said to have been first bred in the parish of Dunlop. A small breed renowned for producing high butterfats, its rich milk was ideal for transforming the area's lush pasture into the local traditional cheese, Dunlop. Moister and crumblier than Cheddar and with a fresher taste, Dunlop was created by Barbara Gilmore in 1688. The cheese was a break from tradition. Historically the area's fare would have been made from skimmed milk, an afterthought from cream and butter production. Barbara taught others the recipe, insisting that Dunlop cheese should be made from 'sweet' (whole) milk.

The name, or appellation, was one of the first assurances of quality in the cheese world, something Ann has sought to build upon. Ann lobbied for and has received PGI (Protected Geographical Indication) status for Traditional Ayrshire Dunlop cheese, an appellation that others are free to claim but only if their cheese is from the designated area, made from the milk of Ayrshire cows and to the traditional and time-consuming farmhouse recipe. To this day Ann remains the sole producer under the PGI, probably due to the lengths to which you must go to create this most Scottish of delicacies.

BONNET

AGE AT RELEASE

6 months

STYLE

Hard

RENNET

Vegetarian

MILK TYPE

Goat: Saanen & Toggenburg

3kg

Drum

TASTING NOTE

A pleasant, clean-flavoured cheese with floral and hazelnut aromas.

WHERE TO BUY

Wholesalers and cheesemongers countrywide. See web for details.

WHAT TO DRINK

Aromatic off-dry whites, light chilled reds, cider and hoppy ales.

DUNLOP

AGE AT RELEASE

6 months

STYLE

Hard

RENNET

Vegetarian

MILK TYPE

Cow: Ayrshire

3kg

Drum

TASTING NOTE

A pungent and creamy mouthful of flavour, including milled seed and Christmas spices that strengthen to seared game and smoke towards the rind.

WHERE TO BUY

Wholesalers and cheesemongers countrywide. See web for details.

WHAT TO DRINK

Medium-bodied reds, sweet whites, malty beer or off-dry cider.

Selina Cairns

ERRINGTONS

In 1981 Humphrey Errington moved his family from Dumfriesshire to the windswept slopes at the foot of the Pentland Hills in Lanarkshire.

As soon as he arrived, he sought ways to add value to the family's cattle and sheep business. He chose cheese and, keen to avoid the bureaucracy of quotas as applied to cow's milk, decided it had to be sheep. A historian by training, he was keen to rekindle tradition and knew the Upper Clyde was once a rich source of sheep's milk cheese. Resolved to settle only for a breed capable of the highest quality cheese, he chose Lacaune, as used for Roquefort, one of the world's most highly prized sheep milk cheeses. Not finding a suitable flock for sale, he set about breeding one for himself, starting with a single sheep and a frozen embryo.

In 1983 cheesemaking began and the result was Lanark Blue, possessing all the quality and some of the spice of Roquefort but unique nonetheless. It is a cheese that changes with the season and faithfully expresses the qualities of the unpasteurised milk according to the age of release, which can be anything from six weeks to eight months.

As the herd grew so did sales and thus the cheesemaking team. The seasonal nature of sheep dairying (most ewes are dry over winter) meant something was needed to maintain continuity of employment. Dunsyre Blue, named after a local town, followed to fill that gap. Made from the purchased milk of a herd of Ayrshire cows, it soon became a best seller. In 2008 a hard ewe's milk cheese, Corra Linn, was added, originally just to make good use of a glut of spring ewe's milk; it is now regarded as one of the finest incarnations of the style.

Selina took over cheesemaking from her father in 2009, and now with husband Andrew (a former civil engineer) managing the flock, runs 300 ewes and a mixed arable enterprise, growing barley as well as producing hay and silage as feed. In 2019 they introduced a herd of goats, solving the problem of year-round milk supply and allowing them to shift the focus to their own milk.

The couple are worthy champions of unpasteurised cheese, having successfully fought and won battles against excessive interpretations of food safety law, and having finessed and even improved the recipes they inherited. Errington is an important slice of Lanarkshire heritage which deserves to be cherished.

CORRA LINN

 AGE AT RELEASE

12 months

STYLE

Hard

RENNET

Vegetarian

MILK TYPE

Sheep: Lacaune

 7.5kg

Drum

TASTING NOTE

12 month version: A concentrated parcel of quartz-cracked aroma: Brazil nut, fig, toffee and polish on the nose, with a ripe and powerful palate of proscuitto game, pan-fried seed and spice. Outstanding.

WHERE TO BUY

Wholesalers and cheesemongers countrywide. See web for details.

WHAT TO DRINK

Rich off-dry whites, chilled tawny port, malty ale.

LANARK BLUE

AGE AT RELEASE

2 months

STYLE

Semi Hard, Blue

RENNET

Vegetarian

MILK TYPE

Sheep: Lacaune

3.5kg

Drum

TASTING NOTE

A crumbly palate of moist, highly-spiced cream and fresh hazelnut flavours.

WHERE TO BUY

Wholesalers and cheesemongers countrywide. See web for details.

WHAT TO DRINK

Semi-sweet and sweet whites.

Cheesemaker Stephen Palmer

THE ETHICAL DAIRY

@theethicaldairy

@theethicaldairy

www.theethicaldairy.co.uk

THE ETHICAL DAIRY

◎ CASTLE DOUGLAS, GALLOWAY

The boldly named Ethical Dairy is turning heads in the dairy world for its stance on farming as well as for the quality of its cheese.

In 2011, when Wilma Finlay asked husband David, whose family had been tenants at Rainton Farm since the 1920s, whether it was possible to keep calves with their mothers, it seemed a naïve question but one that prompted the couple to begin experimenting. The initial trials proved costly, the calves consuming too large a proportion of the milk for the practice to be viable. The farm was losing money, but the couple were set on a course to prove it could be done. Four years later they had found a balance. The calves now have exclusive access to their mothers for the first six weeks, and for the next four months, until they wean, they are separated into nearby pens at 5pm until after the morning's milking, when they return. The morning's milk goes to cheesemaking as well as Cream o' Galloway, the couple's ice cream business.

Volumes are lower than conventional dairy farming, but the couple believe that if the milk goes towards cheese production, higher value can be obtained, and it can be viable. Cheesemaking began in 2014 and volumes are small at present, but a new dairy is near completion that will allow volumes to increase to bring the process to a sustainable level.

Sustainability overall is of paramount importance to the Finlays. The farm has been run organically since the late nineties and they have a 'whole health farming' policy, a holistic mindset that puts the welfare of the herd, environment and staff before profit. David and Wilma believe this approach will pay for itself in the longer term and results are encouraging, with lower instances of mastitis and other illnesses in the cows leading to reduced levels of antibiotics and vet's bills. The cows are living longer and more productive lives and, for those that have experienced the before and after, appear more contented.

It may not be the easy solution, but if the Ethical Dairy can make it work commercially others may follow; something David and Wilma are keen to encourage. They have an open approach to their system and have started an Ethical Food Conference to cross-breed ideas with likeminded farms.

RAINTON TOMME

AGE AT RELEASE

2 months

STYLE

Hard

RENNET

Vegetarian

MILK TYPE

Cow: As other cheeses.

 5kg

 Oval

TASTING NOTE

Sweet floral notes with hints of vanilla and praline at the semi-elastic core and a classy rind of mixed fungi.

WHERE TO BUY

Via the website or wholesalers and cheesemongers countrywide. See web for details.

WHAT TO DRINK

Aromatic off-dry whites, light chilled reds, cider and hoppy ales.

LAGANORY

 AGE AT RELEASE

2 months

STYLE

Semi Hard

RENNET

Vegetarian

MILK TYPE

Cow: Swedish Red
x Montbéliarde x
Holstein

 5kg

 Drum

TASTING NOTE

An enticing musk on the nose with aromas of white
game, cashew and cep with hints of cumin spice. Elastic
palate which quickly yields to a creamy paste full of
multigrain and hay notes at the core, turning richer and
game-like at the rind. Outstanding.

WHERE TO BUY

Via the website or wholesalers and cheesemongers
countrywide. See web for details.

WHAT TO DRINK

Aromatic off-dry whites, light chilled reds, cider and
hoppy ales.

CARRICK

 AGE AT RELEASE

2 months

STYLE

Hard

RENNET

Vegetarian

MILK TYPE

Cow: Swedish Red
x Montbéliarde x
Holstein

 5kg

 Drum

TASTING NOTE

A semi crumbly cheese with flavours of fresh
mushroom and citrus at the core and an earthy rind.

WHERE TO BUY

Via the website or wholesalers and cheesemongers
countrywide. See web for details.

WHAT TO DRINK

Medium-bodied reds, tawny port, sweet whites, malty
beer or off-dry cider.

FLEET VALLEY BLUE

 AGE AT RELEASE

2 months

STYLE

Semi Hard, Blue

RENNET

Vegetarian

MILK TYPE

Cow: Swedish Red
x Montbéliarde x
Holstein

 5kg

 Drum

TASTING NOTE

A characterful cheese with hints of pistachio,
crème caramel and pepper spice at the core, getting
pleasantly wilder at the rind with flavours of dried wild
mushroom, smoke and hung game. Outstanding.

WHERE TO BUY

Via the website or wholesalers and cheesemongers
countrywide. See web for details.

WHAT TO DRINK

Medium to rich reds, tawny port, sweet whites,
medium cider.

Jonny Crickmore

FEN FARM DAIRY

📷 @fenfarmdairy

🐦 @fenfarmdairy

🖳 www.fenfarmdairy.co.uk

FEN FARM DAIRY

With a curd knife and ladle, Jonny Crickmore is taking on the world and winning with his raw milk Brie de Meaux style Baron Bigod.

A cow-mad dynamo from the age of four when he first helped out his father on the family farm, Jonny wanted a way of insulating the family's dairy against the effects of low milk prices, so he thought of cheese. In 2011 he and wife Dulcie turned to Neal's Yard Dairy and in turn French cheesemaking consultant Ivan Larcher, who advised that the place to start would be to swap the herd from one geared to the bulk milk market to one more suitable for cheesemaking. Furthermore, they were told that success lay in creating a cheese only if it fitted a niche, was made from raw milk and in a traditional manner. There was no Brie de Meaux style cheese being made in the UK, so the decision was taken to try and emulate the finest producers of this French gem. Not shy of a challenge, the couple followed the advice, feeling that to compromise might risk long-term failure.

They visited 35 Montbéliarde herds in the Alps to select one that would best suit the rich marshlands of Fen Farm in Suffolk's Waveney Valley. Whilst the area might be topographically the opposite, the breed is also part responsible for cheeses of the lower-lying Epoisses appellation. It was the quality of the milk that was paramount, and the pair knew the smaller yields would suit a high-quality cheese.

Milk and curd require gentle handling to retain complex flavours, so a gravity-fed process was put in place. Also, the curd would be traditionally hand ladled, a time-consuming and costly exercise, but one they knew would help transfer the diverse microflora from their meadows to the cheese without losing character.

Some might question emulating a recipe from overseas rather than helping revive a traditional British style, but as the farm is on land once owned by the Bigods, a powerful Norman family who allied King William in the Conquest of England, the cheese could be said to be true to its heredity and, more significantly, it sits comfortably alongside the few remaining traditional French Brie producers in terms of quality.

BARON BIGOD

AGE AT RELEASE

4 weeks

STYLE

Soft, Bloomy

RENNET

Animal

MILK TYPE

Cow: Montbéliarde

2.5kg, 900g, 250g

Small Disk, Disk

TASTING NOTE

On the nose the rind is a basket of fresh field mushrooms. The palate is rich and brothy with a complex mix of apple, corn-fed chicken, porcini and herb flavours, richening closer to the rind. Outstanding.

WHERE TO BUY

WHAT TO DRINK

Sparkling, chilled light red, dry white, cider.

Kevin Blunt

GOLDEN CROSS CHEESE

🖬 www.goldencrosscheese.co.uk

GOLDEN CROSS CHEESE

Consistency, dedication and experience are three of the critical ingredients in successful cheesemaking. The first two Kevin and Alison Blunt had from the outset and the last they amassed in over thirty years at Golden Cross.

Though not from farming backgrounds, the pair decided to follow a love of animals kindled when Kevin assisted his stepfather on a managed farm during the summer holidays. The couple met at university in the Lake District, both studying biology, he biochemistry, she human biology, but once embarked on their chosen careers all that changed. On a trip to Alison's parents in Eastbourne they spotted a 6-acre plot with a mobile home, which diverted them from a life in laboratories to a smallholding.

A handful of goats, some pigs and a few hens sustained the couple for five years, but in 1989 the retirement of a local cheesemaker to whom they had been selling milk necessitated a change. They bought the business and recipe and the first curd was set for Golden Cross, now one of the country's most sought-after cheeses. Initially based on the Sainte Maure de Touraine, a wrinkly-rinded goats milk log, Golden Cross has become a style of its own, with a character and flavour determined by the raw milk produced from the pastures on the farm.

In 1991, with a new dairy in place and a house built to replace the mobile home, the pair set about increasing the range with a sheep's milk cheese. Assisted in its development by the late James Aldridge, Flower Marie (its name inspired by the Corsican sheep's milk cheese Fleur de Maquis) is made from milk provided by a single flock in Stratford-upon-Avon. As with its sibling, Flower Marie has also become a British classic.

Next generation Matthew Blunt now runs the farm with his parents, supported by a part time team, though this hasn't lessened time with the herd for Kevin, or elbows in the curd for Alison, as their passion remains as strong as at the outset. More awards will no doubt follow, though not serving to promote their brands, as they easily sell all they make, but rather to affirm they are still excelling simply by doing the best they can. These are cheeses it takes effort to source, but the reward is well worth it.

GOLDEN CROSS

 AGE AT RELEASE

2 weeks

STYLE

Fresh, Bloomy

RENNET

Vegetarian

MILK TYPE

Goat: Saanen, Toggenberg

 225g

 Log

TASTING NOTE

Delicate rind with a translucent green mottle and warm dough and button mushroom aromas on the nose. Snow-clean palate with a fudge-like fine grain paste with pressed flower, hayseed and citrus flavours. Outstanding.

WHERE TO BUY

Wholesalers and cheesemongers countrywide. See website.

WHAT TO DRINK

Sparkling, aromatic whites, light reds, hoppy ale and cider.

FLOWER MARIE

AGE AT RELEASE

2 weeks

STYLE

Soft, Bloomy

RENNET

Vegetarian

MILK TYPE

Sheep: Friesland-Dorset

200g, 600g

Square

TASTING NOTE

An elegant rind of soft, downy penicillin with some breakdown beneath. The core gives high-tone blossom and rice pudding notes with a hint of cox apple. The palate combines lime acidity, hay and chestnut mushroom from the lactic core, and fresh bread and game notes from the rind. Exceptional.

WHERE TO BUY

Wholesalers and cheesemongers countrywide. See website.

WHAT TO DRINK

Sparkling, aromatic whites, light reds, hoppy ale and cider.

CHABIS

AGE AT RELEASE

2 weeks

STYLE

Fresh, Bloomy

RENNET

Vegetarian

MILK TYPE

Goat: Saanen, Toggenberg

65g

Button

TASTING NOTE

The young rind emits notes of fresh field mushroom, clean grass and fresh cream. The super-fine-grain palate harbours a vivid palette of flavours from milled seed, freshly cut cep and hung white game closer to the rind. Outstanding.

WHERE TO BUY

Wholesalers and cheesemongers countrywide. See website.

WHAT TO DRINK

Sparkling, aromatic whites, light reds, hoppy ale and cider.

Bruce Rowan

GOODWOOD

GOODWOOD

Home Farm at Goodwood has been supplying produce for the Dukes and Duchesses of Richmond for over 300 years. Set on free-draining chalk at the foot of the South Downs, the farm is positioned at the heart of the 12,000-acre Goodwood Estate, a spot blessed with a unique microclimate suited to spring barley, fodder and the rich grasses on which the estate's herd of dairy Shorthorns graze. Shorthorn cows are one of the breeds native to the British Isles. Their low yields, rich in butterfats and protein, make them an ideal source for cheesemaking milk, a process which began on the estate in 2010.

Cheesemaker Bruce Rowan, a Philadelphian restaurateur who'd established roots in England during his five-year tenure at Neal's Yard Dairy and a two-year stint as cheesemaker at Quicke's Farm, was drawn to Goodwood by the quality of the milk and its organic nature. The Duchess of Richmond, a pioneer of the organic movement, developed the first 100% organically-fed dairy in the UK and was a founder member of the Soil Association.

Bruce took over at the vat in 2012, at a time when their first cheese, Charlton, named after a village within the estate, was just entering the market. A farmhouse cheese made to a Cheddar recipe, it was successful from the start, though Bruce sought greater consistency, always an issue in the first years of a long maturing cheese. He also wanted to launch new creations. Both ambitions he has achieved. Charlton is a Cheddar equal to many of the finest, and Levin Down and Molcombe blue, two soft mould-ripened cheeses, now extend a broader cheeseboard offering from the estate.

Bruce almost singlehandedly crafts 11 tonnes of cheese a year in the dairy, just a short walk from the parlour. Production will likely remain at these levels, as the primary aim is to provide small volumes of high-quality cheese to serve at the estate's prestigious horseracing and motorsport events, as well as in the hotel, restaurant and cafés. The cheeses have also breached the estate's flint-walled boundaries in a limited way and can be found in a small number of local delicatessens or directly via wholesale. As with many of the best artisan cheeses, don't expect Goodwood's to jump out at you. They must be sought. As their availability hides in the stunning chalk-green folds of the South Downs National Park, half the fun lies in the chase.

LEVIN DOWN

 AGE AT RELEASE

4 weeks

STYLE

Soft Bloomy

RENNET

Vegetarian

MILK TYPE

Cow: Shorthorn

 250g

 Small Disk

TASTING NOTE

A clean, chunky rind gives way to a cool palate of fresh lactic flavours: mushroom, grass and lemon with a hint of salted butter. Outstanding.

WHERE TO BUY

Wholesalers and cheesemongers locally. See web for details.

WHAT TO DRINK

Off-dry sparkling or white, light & fruity red.

MOLCOMB BLUE

AGE AT RELEASE
4 weeks

STYLE
Soft, Blue

RENNET
Vegetarian

MILK TYPE
Cow: Shorthorn

250g

Small Disk

TASTING NOTE
The pretty mottled rind covers a buttery core threaded with mild pepper spice and butter-sweated mushroom flavours. The rind, worth approaching separately, is a basket of foraged fungus and dried meats. Outstanding.

WHERE TO BUY
Wholesalers and cheesemongers locally. See web for details.

WHAT TO DRINK
Sweet whites, chilled tawny port, rich ales.

CHARLTON

AGE AT RELEASE
12 months

STYLE
Hard

RENNET
Vegetarian

MILK TYPE
Cow: Shorthorn

10kg

Drum

TASTING NOTE
A rich nose of toffee and popcorn with hints of salted cashew leads to a gentler, creamy palate of field mushroom and milled grain, turning to lichen and stone at the rind.

WHERE TO BUY
Wholesalers and cheesemongers locally. See web for details.

WHAT TO DRINK
Sweet whites, rich reds, vintage port, malty ale, cider, whisky.

John Bourne

H S BOURNE

H S BOURNE

As a maker of Cheshire cheese, HS Bourne has pedigree. The family can trace its heritage as traditional crafters of this endangered territorial back to 1750, and since 1930 on Bank Farm. In their time they have seen the makers around them disappear as the popularity of this friable, farm-produced delicacy has faded in favour of mass-produced Cheshire that more often resembles chalk than cheese.

A crumbly cheese with a loose texture, Cheshire's popularity is said to have developed earlier than others due to the salt springs that run under the rich Cheshire pastures, giving the cheese a distinctive saline tang. It was one of the earliest named styles of cheese in the UK and the most popular until the 1930s, but the advent of centralised marketing and distribution by the Milk Marketing Board, and the pressures of World War Two, turned it into a commodity and the farmhouse tradition all but died out.

John Bourne has overseen the vat since 1958, assisted since 2000 by cheesemaker Paul Barron. They make a range of waxed and clothbound Cheshires, both red (with annatto colouring) and white, true to family recipes developed over generations. John has added blue to the palette. Blue Cheshire, as with many penicillin-influenced cheeses, would have originated as a fortuitous accident. Subsequently, In an effort to repeat this unintended delight, cheesemakers would have found ways of encouraging the style by maturing these loose-knit cheeses in proximity to environments rich in mould spores, such as a tack room or boot store. Next generation Hugo Bourne is helping to steer the style from his tractor seat, his passion for soil management and experiments with grass types bolstering the continued development of this classic.

MATURE CHESHIRE

STYLE
Semi Hard

RENNET
Vegetarian

MILK TYPE
Cow: Friesian

 Drum

TASTING NOTE

A crumbly core that gives clotted cream and farmyard aromas.

WHERE TO BUY

Farm shop, online or wholesalers and cheesemongers countrywide. See web for details.

WHAT TO DRINK

Mid-bodied reds, semi-sweet whites, malty beer or off-dry cider.

BLUE CHESHIRE

STYLE
Semi Hard, Blue

RENNET
Vegetarian

MILK TYPE
Cow: Friesian

 9kg

Drum

TASTING NOTE
A mid-strength cheese with peppery blue tang and mineral and cream core.

WHERE TO BUY
Farm shop, online or wholesalers and cheesemongers countrywide. See web for details.

WHAT TO DRINK
Rich reds, tawny port, sweet whites and dessert gin.

Stacey Hedges

HAMPSHIRE CHEESES

@tunworth_cheese

@TunworthCheese

www.hampshirecheeses.co.uk

HAMPSHIRE CHEESES

⊙ HERRIARD, HAMPSHIRE

When in 2003 Stacey Hedges set out to find a cheese that would fill a gap in the UK market, little did she think she would create one hailed by some experts as the world's best example of its type.

The secret to her success was a thoroughness of approach fuelled by passion. The motivation for Stacey had been kindled working in a cheese shop in her native Sydney, but it wasn't until her move to the UK and meeting a dairy farmer at the gates of her children's school that the passion took flame. She began by making cheese at home. Throughout the trial process she consulted Randolph Hodgson of wholesaler Neal's Yard, who helped her understand production as well as the marketplace, the latter an essential consideration for a successful recipe. She was emphatically told the main criterion was that 'it had to be as good as the best'.

In 2005 family encouragement to turn professional necessitated a move. The following year, Tunworth, named after a local hamlet, won Supreme Champion at the British Cheese Awards. Calls from retailers followed and demand could easily have pressured Hampshire Cheeses to scale up immediately, but consistency was the priority and a plan of slow growth ensued. Charlotte Spruce joined Stacey as cheesemaker in 2006 and in 2010 Hampshire Cheeses moved to its current premises where they now make up to 800 Tunworths a day. Charlotte has added her own creation to the range, Winslade, a spruce-wrapped cross between Camembert and Vacherin. They are faithful to the original advice, that it must be as good as the best. In sourcing high-grade milk from a single herd, sticking to a slow acidification make (a pain for commercial producers) and hand ladling, they have ensured that, despite continued growth, Tunworth remains true to its origins and is a yardstick by which PDO Camembert should be judged.

TUNWORTH

 AGE AT RELEASE

4 weeks

STYLE

Soft, Bloomy

RENNET

Animal

MILK TYPE

Cow: Holstein
Friesian

 250g

 Small Disk

TASTING NOTE

A Camembert style true to type with wild mushroom
and game notes on the nose and fermented cabbage
and mushroom broth flavours from the creamy core.
Outstanding.

WHERE TO BUY

Via website or wholesalers and cheesemongers
countrywide. See web for details.

WHAT TO DRINK

Sparkling, aromatic whites, light reds, hoppy ale and
cider.

WINSLADE

 AGE AT RELEASE

4 weeks

STYLE

Soft, Bloomy

RENNET

Animal

MILK TYPE

Cow: Holstein
Friesian

 250g

 Small Disk

TASTING NOTE

This cross between a Camembert and Vacherin has
fresh mushroom and white game aromas on the
nose that darken on the palate with sweet notes of
undergrowth, chanterelle and hints of juniper closer
the the spruce banding.

WHERE TO BUY

Via website or wholesalers and cheesemongers
countrywide. See web for details.

WHAT TO DRINK

Sparkling, aromatic whites, light reds, cider and hoppy
ale.

Mark Hardy

HIGH WEALD DAIRY

⊙ HORSTED KEYNES, WEST SUSSEX

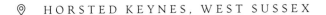

If anyone aspires to the life of a cheesemaker but is concerned about long-term success, the protean Mark Hardy and High Weald Dairy would be fine inspiration. As is said, there are no secrets to success but fathomable reasons. In Mark's case it is a combination of a questing mind, adaptability and a good team. He and wife Sarah have developed a thriving business in the Ashdown Forest from small beginnings. At the heart of their range lie the dairy's sheep's milk cheeses.

Now made from the bought-in milk of a local flock, their recipes stem from High Weald's foundation in 1986, when Mark and his parents started milking sheep at their home in Duddleswell to supply a cheese producer. They soon found that volume exceeded requirements so began crafting their own cheese, initially finding a willing market for a Halloumi style within London's Cypriot community.

The sheep have gone, but in 2003 the business moved to its current premises, on a farm owned by Mark's family, allowing them a plentiful supply of British Friesian milk as well as a place to connect with their community. As the cheese range has grown, the focus for Mark and Sarah has remained local, a desire to connect with their customers a priority that makes sense in terms of profitability as well as lifestyle, as to craft a product and never experience it being appreciated is the lot of many a farmer. The couple run cheese courses within a converted barn on site whose eves regularly witness the warmth of dinners and public events, something that requires much effort and late nights, though for the mindful cheesemaker there is the realisation that a happy customer is for life and not just for dinner.

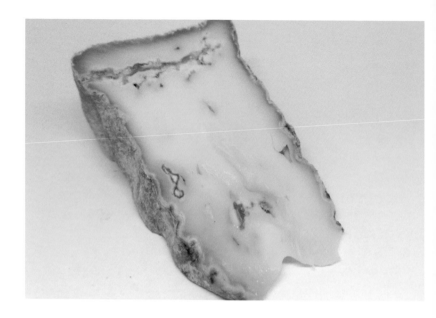

BRIGHTON EWE

 AGE AT RELEASE
3 months

STYLE
Semi Soft, Blue

RENNET
Vegetarian

MILK TYPE
Sheep

3.8kg

Drum

TASTING NOTE

Pleasing spiced walnut and cream notes on the nose and a semi-firm palate giving dried orchard fruit and nuanced blue spice. Outstanding.

WHERE TO BUY

Farm shop, via website or wholesalers and cheesemongers countrywide. See web for details.

WHAT TO DRINK

Rich reds, tawny port, sweet whites and dessert gin.

BRIGHTON BLUE

AGE AT RELEASE

3 months

STYLE

Semi Hard, Blue

RENNET

Vegetarian

MILK TYPE

Cow: Holstein
Friesian

 3.8kg

Drum

TASTING NOTE

Creamy, giving and pleasant, with cream of mushroom
soup flavours threaded with a mid-strength blue spice.

WHERE TO BUY

Farm shop, via website or wholesalers and
cheesemongers countrywide. See web for details.

WHAT TO DRINK

Rich reds, tawny port, sweet whites and dessert gin.

Rory Stone

HIGHLAND FINE CHEESES

Rory Stone presides over more than 60 years of cheesemaking at Highland Fine Cheeses and is still to be found elbows-deep in curd daily, despite running a £1.5 million business employing 16 people.

Rory grew up on Blairlath Farm, where the dairy now stands, nestled between the heather-clad slopes and wind-whipped Durnoch Firth on the outskirts of Tain. In the early fifties his father, Reggie, complained that he could no longer buy Crowdie, a cheese once ubiquitous in the Highlands.

Until the beginning of the 20th century many smallholdings would have had a cow and, after skimming off the cream for butter, its milk would be left to sour in the churn near a fireplace. The following morning the whey would be drained off through a cloth sack, and the curd scrambled and salted. The result, Crowdie, was eaten fresh or rolled in oatmeal.

Rory's mother, Susannah, acquainted with this tradition, once took a churn aside from the morning's milking of their 14 dairy shorthorn cows and made some in the bathtub with the help of a little lactic acid bacteria donated by the local chemist. The five kilos produced were too much for the family, so a fledgling business was born. Caboc followed, a rich cheese, similar in production to Crowdie, but made from cream. Its choice was not without provenance, Susannah being a descendent of Mariota de Ile, originator of the recipe in 15th century.

These cheeses, as well as others fresh and flavoured, were a hit, but as styles easy to replicate on a larger scale, they soon found imitators. By the early 1990s the company was struggling against the mass market. Having worked briefly at the dairy after leaving school, Rory returned on the basis that he would run the company. He decided to work with purchased milk and, alongside the traditional cheeses, he introduced others varied enough to complete any cheeseboard, including brie, camembert and Cheddar styles, as well as blues. Having farmed Shorthorns, he understood that milk quality was the key and he now buys from three small farms, each with small breeds, helping to keep the herds viable.

Dry-witted and with a keen desire to stimulate discussion, Rory has named his latest creations Minger (a pungent washed-rind) and Fat Cow (a large Alpine cheese), to the effect that it has generated significant interest in Scotland. Such marketing is bold and might backfire should the product itself disappoint. However, Rory's desire to innovate his frenetic work ethic and extensive experience have placed the quality of his creations beyond reproach.

MORANGIE BRIE

AGE AT RELEASE
2 weeks

STYLE
Soft, Bloomy

RENNET
Vegetarian

MILK TYPE
Cow

1kg, 250g

Small Disk

TASTING NOTE
A richly flavoured creamy cheese with sweet crème brulée notes and a saline tang.

WHERE TO BUY
Wholesalers and cheesemongers countrywide. See web for details.

WHAT TO DRINK
Sparkling, aromatic whites, light reds, hoppy ale and cider.

MINGER

 AGE AT RELEASE
3 weeks

STYLE
Soft, Washed Rind

RENNET
Vegetarian

MILK TYPE
Cow

 250g

Tile

TASTING NOTE
Pleasantly minging with mid-wild mushroom and game aromas and a putty-like texture on the palate with gentler flavours of creamy peanut.

WHERE TO BUY
Wholesalers and cheesemongers countrywide. See web for details.

WHAT TO DRINK
Aromatic off-dry white, light red, malty ale or medium cider.

FAT COW

 AGE AT RELEASE

2 months

STYLE

Hard

RENNET

Vegetarian

MILK TYPE

Cow

6kg

Wheel

TASTING NOTE

A sweet Alpine nose with notes of singed cream and toast. On the palate an elastic core gives flavours of hay and dried mushroom.

WHERE TO BUY

Wholesalers and cheesemongers countrywide. See web for details.

WHAT TO DRINK

Rich whites, semi-sweet whites, chilled reds, off-dry cider, malty ale.

BLUE MURDER

 AGE AT RELEASE

3 months

STYLE

Semi Soft, Blue

RENNET

Vegetarian

MILK TYPE

Cow

650g

Square

TASTING NOTE

A unique sweet curd nose with hints of toffee over mixed spice and a creamy, fresh palate balancing spice and cream.

WHERE TO BUY

Wholesalers and cheesemongers countrywide. See web for details.

WHAT TO DRINK

Medium to rich reds, tawny port, sweet whites, medium cider.

Becky Holden

HOLDEN FARM DAIRY

:camera: @hafodcheese
:bird: @hafodcheese
:file: www.hafodcheese.co.uk

HOLDEN FARM DAIRY

There are few better examples of the medium of cheese reflecting the uniqueness of a farm ecosystem through the palate than Holden Farm Dairy's Hafod Cheese. Patrick and Becky Holden have been nurturing the farm's 300 acres organically since 1973. It is now the longest established organic dairy farm in Wales.

The origins of Hafod (Welsh for summer pasture) go back to 2005, when Randolph Hodgson, the then chair of the Specialist Cheesemakers Association, asked Patrick if he could bring a group of leading cheesemakers for a walk around the farm as a backdrop for a discussion about the influence of native breeds and organic farming on cheese quality. After the visit, Patrick had a talk with his son Sam and partner Rachel, asking whether they would be interested in using some of the farm's milk for cheese making. The answer was yes and the first cheese was made in August 2007, enabling the potential of the farm's 'taste of place' to be unlocked.

The current Hafod recipe has benefited from various influences. These include a 1917 imprint of Dora Saker's Practical Cheddar Cheese Making, the Swiss mountain cheeses of the Alpage via pioneer maker Dougal Campbell (a long-time friend of Patrick), and Simon Jones of Lincolnshire Poacher. Collectively these equipped the couple to make a cheese exhibiting the unique qualities of the farm's milk.

Striving for quality over quantity, a long make-time was decided upon, ensuring the velvety, buttery character particular to Hafod. The cheese's complex taste is the fusion of the milk from the Ayrshire cattle, years of nurturing soil and pasture diversity, and the myriad microbes channelling flavour to the palate. Sensitive, inquisitive and deliberately non-interventional cheesemaking habits play their part too.

Sam and Rachel have moved on to pastures new and the management of the dairy is now overseen by Patrick and Becky, maintaining the interconnected nature of the farming and cheesemaking. The continuing spirit of enquiry has resulted in developments which include 'Hafod Sauvage', a trial cheese made without the use of bought-in starter culture (the lactic acid-producing bacteria added to most cheeses to acidify the curd), instead allowing the milk's own microflora to do the job. Latterly, following a year of trials, they have moved to cloth-less Hafod with a natural rind, which is thought to increase the capacity of the maturing cheese to interact with its local environment, allowing an even greater expression of the Holden Farm soil.

HAFOD

AGE AT RELEASE

16 months

STYLE

Hard

RENNET

Animal

MILK TYPE

Cow: Ayrshire

10kg, 18kg

Large Drum

TASTING NOTE

The core, enjoyed first, has a smooth paste giving flavours of porcini broth, seeded bread pudding, cashew and hay. The rind, a shame to avoid, adds the pungency of a warm autumnal forest. Outstanding.

WHERE TO BUY

Wholesalers and cheesemongers countrywide. See website.

WHAT TO DRINK

Sweet whites, rich reds, tawny port, malty ale, strong cider.

Tim Homewood and Angela Morris

HOMEWOOD CHEESES

:camera: @homewoodcheeses

:bird: @homewoodcheeses

:window: www.homewoodcheeses.co.uk

HOMEWOOD CHEESES

⊙ UBLEY, SOMERSET

Tim Homewood and Angela Morris met at Bristol's thriving Tobacco Factory Market, him working a stall for Peter Humphreys at White Lake Cheese and her selling homemade cakes and chocolate.

Bound by a love of food, they began making a little cheese at home, but this allowed little scope for Tim's experience (he'd also worked as a trainee at Bath Soft Cheese), so it was time to take the relationship with cheese further. In 2008 they started renting a unit in Shepton Mallet that had been used for yoghurt production. A meeting with the Dorset sheep farmer who had been supplying it with milk set the course for their recipes and the pair started trials to find a niche. The Cypriot classic, Halloumi, a cooking cheese traditionally made from Mouflon sheep's milk (but now largely cow's or goat's) was where the pair started. The curd for the cheese is heated in the whey and then kneaded, giving the cheese a springy, squeaky texture that uniquely does not melt when heated. A little bland when eaten raw, the sweet flavours come to the fore when slices are barbequed or shallow- fried.

A Feta-style pickled ewe's milk cheese followed. Feta, a simple shepherd's or goatherd's cheese, has been made in the same way since long before its mention in Homer's Odyssey. The curds are left to drain in bags, or lightly pressed, before being salted, cut into blocks and immersed in brine until the cheese is required. As with Halloumi, Tim and Angela's pickled ewe's milk cheese is an ingredient rather than a table cheese, something that sets them apart from most artisan cheesemakers in Somerset. They quickly found a following with quality-conscious chefs in the area. Fresh cheese and ricotta (meaning re-cooked, made by heating whey post cheesemaking and skimming off curd grains which are then moulded and eaten fresh) were next, Tim and Angela aware that their culinary customers might be keen to take several products, something less likely if they were selling table cheeses.

Aveline and Old Demdyke broke the mould, but much still ends up in discerning West Country dining establishments; partly by design, as to dine well while visiting customers is a sensible part of any cheesemaker's business plan.

AVELINE

AGE AT RELEASE

6 weeks

STYLE

Soft, Bloomy

RENNET

Vegetarian

MILK TYPE

Sheep: Friesland

 150g

 Polo Mint

TASTING NOTE

The mushroomy rind yields with a spring to reveal a putty-like, sweet-sheep core with notes of fresh grass, lime and grapefruit.

WHERE TO BUY

Wholesalers and cheesemongers in the South. See web for details.

WHAT TO DRINK

Sparkling, aromatic whites, light chilled reds, cider & crisp ale.

Brendan and Garth Reade

ISLE OF MULL CHEESE

———————————

A short walk up a hill from the kaleidoscopically vibrant Tobermory lies a rich source of pleasure for the cheese lover; one that would not exist but for the vision and resilience of a family originally from Somerset.

On holiday in 1981 Christine and Jeff Reade took this same Isle of Mull walk and encountered a husk of a smallholding, roofless and without power. What was a break from the travails of running a West Country dairy farm led to hours on motorways, building a dream and relocating a young family to where Jeff and Christine felt their skills might better develop a niche.

No one was serving the community with local milk, and in the lush maritime pastures they saw a squandered resource, rich year-round feed for their herd. At first cheese was a sideline, something to mop up winter milk when the tourists had left, but in 2000 they took the decision to divert all their milk into the production of Isle of Mull. This was in part due to inconsistencies with the milk quota system, but also because it would allow them to avoid what they saw as the indignity of pasteurising, a practice they had reluctantly adopted following legislative pressure.

The farm makes two cheeses, each unpasteurised and attaining the heights of which each style is capable. Isle of Mull, a Cheddar recipe which is cloth-bound and then larded through maturation, is one of Cheddar's punchiest incarnations. The other, Hebridean Blue, is similar in style to a Stilton, though unpasteurised. Both vary naturally throughout the year both in colour and flavour depending on feed, but there is no variability in quality.

The farm is now in the hands of Jeff and Christine's sons, cheesemaker Brendan and herdsman Garth, and their families. Their cheeses, whilst counted among the most highly regarded in the industry, are only a part of the operation which alone wouldn't allow such a remote farm to flourish. A café and holiday cottages contribute, as does a 60 strong herd of pigs (willing devourers of the whey from cheese production) as well as meat sales and energy generation.

A paragon of sustainability, the farm produces 150% of the energy it requires from wind and water turbines. Moreover, the heat taken from the evening milk in the process of chilling it for storage overnight is itself captured in a heat storage tank and used to help bring the milk back to temperature for the morning's make. At Isle of Mull there's innovation at every turn: the heat storage tank beneath the dairy looks, to the uninitiated, like a swimming pool, perhaps the world's first to be grass-heated.

HEBRIDEAN BLUE

 AGE AT RELEASE

3 months

STYLE

Semi Hard, Blue

RENNET

Animal

MILK TYPE

Cow: As for Cheddar

 7kg

Cylinder

TASTING NOTE

Full-bodied, pungent and saline with a pepper spice and hints of smoky cream.

WHERE TO BUY

Via the website or wholesalers and cheesemongers countrywide. See web for details.

WHAT TO DRINK

Rich reds, port, sweet whites and sweet cider.

CHEDDAR

 AGE AT RELEASE

10 months

STYLE

Hard

RENNET

Animal

MILK TYPE

Cow: Brown Swiss
Friesian, Jersey,
Norweigan Red,
Swedish Red,

 25kg

 Large Drum

TASTING NOTE

Brooding, powerful and direct, the palate conjures a
pan full of venison and butter-fried almond flavours
with a chilli-bite that softens to subtle and lingering
notes of truffle and spice. Outstanding.

WHERE TO BUY

Via the website or wholesalers and cheesemongers
countrywide. See web for details.

WHAT TO DRINK

Sweet whites, rich reds, vintage port, malty ale, cider,
whisky.

Richard Hodgson

ISLE OF WIGHT CHEESE

[instagram] @theiowcheeseco
[twitter] @theiowcheeseco
[web] www.isleofwightcheese.co.uk

ISLE OF WIGHT CHEESE

———————

Once well-trodden by Channel Island breeds, the pastures of the Isle of Wight are now home to only eleven milking dairies in total, down from thirty in 2006 when Julie Hodgson first hit on the idea of cheesemaking.

At the time there were no cheesemakers at all, something Julie, a hotelier, resolved to remedy after discussions with her chef. He moved on but the idea stuck, and in 2007 her son, Richard, then 26, resigned as a TV editor in the North East and started the project with a quest to find the right milk.

Queen Bower Dairy's farm in the tranquil Arreton Valley had been supplying Guernsey milk to towns on the east of the island since 1931, but times were now difficult. Competition, milk round costs and a low milk price for the surplus meant that the additional value gained from having a cheesemaker would help. Thus the Isle of Wight Cheese Company was born.

Richard took a course at Reaseheath College in Nantwich under Val Bines and, after building the cheeseemaking dairy at Queen Bower in a pair of barns, production of Isle of Wight Blue and Isle of Wight Soft began. By Richard's own account, the first batches were below expectations but by batch 16 the quality was high enough to see the Isle of Wight Blue win a gold at the World Cheese Awards. Whilst the commercial proposition at Queen Bower farm had improved, in 2017 the farmer sought retirement and, with no successor, the farm was put up for sale. Richard, keen to ensure the quality and control of his milk supply, took the snap decision to buy the farm. He knew he would need to convert all the milk into cheese to make the figures work.

As with cheesemaking, Richard took to farming with considerable drive and a desire to develop the milk with a focus on quality, though the role of farmer and cheesemaker became unsustainable so after two years the cows were sold to a farm from which Richard now sources his milk.

The company is most widely known for its first pair of cheeses, The Isle of Wight Blue and Isle of Wight Soft, as it is only these that leave the island in any significant volume. The others are made in smaller quantities for local outlets. Make the effort to seek out Richard's lesser known creations and you will be rewarded with cheeses as visually tantalising as they are tasty; the striking blue-green-rippled rind of Blue Slipper is particularly evocative of its surroundings.

ISLE OF WIGHT SOFT

 AGE AT RELEASE
3 weeks

STYLE
Soft, Bloomy

RENNET
Vegetarian

MILK TYPE
Cow: Guernsey, Jersey

 200g

Small Drum

TASTING NOTE
A nose of singed cream over white game and hints of caramel leads to a melt–in-the-mouth creamy palate full of pan-fried seed, cep and hazelnut flavours. Outstanding.

WHERE TO BUY
Wholesalers and cheesemongers countrywide. See web for details.

WHAT TO DRINK
Off-dry sparkling or white, light & fruity red.

BORTHWOOD

AGE AT RELEASE

3 weeks

STYLE

Soft, Bloomy

RENNET

Vegetarian

MILK TYPE

Cow: Guernsey, Jersey

200g

Small Disk

TASTING NOTE

High hazelnut, salted cream and field mushroom notes from the runny core.

WHERE TO BUY

Wholesalers and cheesemongers countrywide. See web for details.

WHAT TO DRINK

Sparkling, aromatic whites, light reds, hoppy ale and cider.

BLUE SLIPPER

AGE AT RELEASE

3 weeks

STYLE

Soft, Bloomy

RENNET

Vegetarian

MILK TYPE

Cow: Guernsey, Jersey

200g

Small Disk

TASTING NOTE

Rich saline cream from the core and pungent dried fruits, wild mushroom and pepper from the rind.

WHERE TO BUY

Wholesalers and cheesemongers countrywide. See web for details.

WHAT TO DRINK

Medium to rich reds, tawny port, sweet whites, medium cider.

GALLYBAGGER

AGE AT RELEASE

5 months

STYLE

Hard

RENNET

Vegetarian

MILK TYPE

Cow: Guernsey, Jersey

5kg

Drum

TASTING NOTE

Lovely toffee, popcorn and pan-fried wild mushroom aromas. On the palate a gently elastic break leads to flavours of hazelnut, prosciutto and sweet cream.

WHERE TO BUY

Wholesalers and cheesemongers countrywide. See web for details.

WHAT TO DRINK

Rich reds, sweet whites, malty beer, cider.

ISLE OF WIGHT BLUE

AGE AT RELEASE

4 weeks

STYLE

Soft, Blue

RENNET

Vegetarian

MILK TYPE

Cow: Guernsey, Jersey

 200g

 Small Drum

TASTING NOTE

A good balance of spiced mushroom from the blue piercing the salted cream, cashew and meaty notes from the core. Darker, smokier and spicier at the rind. Outstanding.

WHERE TO BUY

Wholesalers and cheesemongers countrywide. See web for details.

WHAT TO DRINK

Light to medium reds, sherry, sweet whites, medium cider.

Bill Oglethorpe

KAPPACASEIN DAIRY

@ @kappacasein

𝕏 @kappacasein

▭ www.kappacasein.com

KAPPACASEIN DAIRY

⊚   BERMONDSEY, LONDON

For over a thousand years, ever since Roman feet first crossed London Bridge, the area to its south has been one of the country's most important food trading hubs. And so Borough Market remains today, where office workers and tourists jostle for fare from across the globe, few knowing that its most local food is cheese. Formed in 2008 just over a mile away in Bermondsey, Kappacasein Dairy crafts its curd beneath two cavernous Victorian railway arches carrying trains towards Kent, a journey by van that Bill Oglethorpe makes four times weekly when collecting milk from their supplier, an organic dairy farm in Sevenoaks.

There are few people more inquisitive or dedicated to their craft in British cheese than Bill, who recounts his story with a modesty as if you might have heard it all before. It's one where a Swiss missionary spots the son of a Church friend, encourages him to study agriculture in Switzerland, which takes him to make cheese in Provence, leading in turn to a position at Borough's Neal's Yard Dairy, who assist him in setting up his own ground-breaking cheesemaking dairy close-by.

The same gentle nature pervades his cheesemaking. The milk is transported from the farm unpasteurised and still warm, the starter cultures already gently at work, before being transferred, without pumping, to the dairy's 19th century 500-litre copper vat. Once the milk is to temperature the rennet is added and, soon after, the curd is cut to grain-sized pieces with a cheese harp, using the action of a leisurely rower's arm. Once settled the curds are fished out with a hooped muslin bag and transferred to waiting moulds to create one of the dairy's two main cheeses.

The dairy's signature cheese, Bermondsey Hard-Pressed, is modelled on a classical Gruyère d'Alpage. After pressing, the wheels are washed and turned weekly on spruce shelves in the adjoining railway arch and matured for between six and twelve months. Their Raclette, made to a moister recipe and aged for shorter periods, is mostly destined for Raclette machines dispensing bubbling cheese onto baby potatoes and cornichons, but it provides a great table cheese if aged for longer.

Bermonsey Friar, made to an Italian formaggio cotto recipe, is made for frying and, along with ricotta and yoghurt, provides local chefs and cooks with authentic London-sourced ingredients for their dishes. Much of the cheese however makes the short journey to the dairy's stall and shop in Borough Market, the spot where foodies have bought, sold and gorged upon local produce for over a millennium.

RACLETTE

AGE AT RELEASE

3 months

STYLE

Hard

RENNET

Animal

MILK TYPE

Cow: H.F.,
Montbéliarde,
Swedish Red

18kg

Large Wheel

TASTING NOTE

Nice bounce to the core which breaks emitting aromas of ground nut and light spice in butter. Richer and more organic on the palate with rich grass and warm walnut notes. Outstanding.

WHERE TO BUY

Wholesalers and cheesemongers in London. See web for details.

WHAT TO DRINK

Aromatic whites, chilled reds, dry cider, hoppy ale.

BERMONDSEY
HARD PRESSED

AGE AT RELEASE

6 months

STYLE

Hard

RENNET

Animal

MILK TYPE

Cow: H.F.,
Montbéliarde,
Swedish Red

24kg

Large Wheel

TASTING NOTE

Firm bounce-crack to the core with high-tone aromas
of crushed Brazil nuts and crème caramel continuing
on the palate, mingling with dried mushroom and
mineral notes towards the rind. Outstanding.

WHERE TO BUY

Wholesalers and cheesemongers in London. See web
for details.

WHAT TO DRINK

Rich whites, medium-bodied reds, off-dry cider, malty
ale.

Nick Keen

KEEN'S CHEDDAR

 @keensCheddar

 www.keensCheddar.co.uk

KEEN'S CHEDDAR

◉ WINCANTON, SOMERSET

In comparison with Cheddar made by vast machines speedily forcing pasteurised milk into uniform, vacuum-packed blocks, only a crumb gives an inkling of the wonders the style is capable of.

The town of Cheddar and its nearby Gorge and caves were once the source of many hundreds of different farmhouse Somerset Cheddars, a number that had been slashed to a handful during World War Two. At one point only a pair, Montgomery's and Keen's, were still producing traditionally Cheddared, unpasteurised, cloth-bound incarnations. They have since been joined by others, but the Keen family can claim continuity as no other.

The 500-acre Moorhayes Farm, nestled in the Blackmore Vale north of Wincanton, has been home to the Keen family since 1899 when John Bridle bought the property. Now under fourth generation George and Stephen and fifth generation James and Nick Keen, they continue to transform the rich pastureland into their signature cheeses, sticking to production principles that remain largely unchanged.

Milk arrives into the 5,500 vat from the dairy 50 yards away and is inoculated with traditional pint-pot starter cultures and rennet to produce junket. The junket is then cut, before being heated to 41°C, the warmth assisting the development of acidity and dryness in the resulting curd. It is then drained and 'pitched' onto a draining table before being hand-Cheddared (cut into blocks and stacked to texturise and further advance whey drainage and acidity development) and then milled. At Keen's the cheeses are pressed for three days and bathed in hot water, a process that gives them their signature crumbly texture. They are then larded and clothed before being coated in a thin breathable membrane to discourage the unwanted attention of cheese mites.

To make such cheeses instead of commercially produced Cheddar requires levels of labour and attention that are scant reflected or recouped by any elevation in price, meaning that it is only the passionate who undertake such a route. Efforts have been made to highlight the value-added difference to the consumer, but few have come close to public enlightenment. The Slow Food Presidia organisation is the best guide, stating that 'Artisan Somerset Cheddar' must be unpasteurised, use pint-pot starters, be hand Cheddared, not shrink wrapped, and aged for a minimum of 11 months. Keen's, along with Montgomery and Westcombe, are committed members, but thankfully for the cheese lover, if not the producers, this elevation to what amounts to a 'grand cru' of cheese has had little effect on affordability. Their cheeses are currently among the most undervalued of artisan produce. A treat at any price.

CHEDDAR

AGE AT RELEASE
12 months

STYLE
Hard

RENNET
Animal

MILK TYPE
Cow: Friesian,
Normandy, Swedish
Red,

 25kg

 Large Drum

TASTING NOTE
A beefy monster with a piquant chilli spice running through brothy mushroom and brown game flavours. Persistent and lingering.

WHERE TO BUY
Wholesalers and cheesemongers countrywide. See web for details.

WHAT TO DRINK
Sweet whites, rich reds, vintage port, malty ale, cider, whisky.

EXTRA MATURE

 AGE AT RELEASE

18 months

STYLE

Hard

RENNET

Animal

MILK TYPE

Cow: Friesian,
Normandy, Swedish
Red,

 25kg

Large Drum

TASTING NOTE

The brittle core releases aromas of toasted nut and
boiling custard, hiding a chilli-punch on the palate
which recedes to notes of wild mushroom and dried
fruits. Outstanding.

WHERE TO BUY

Wholesalers and cheesemongers countrywide. See web
for details.

WHAT TO DRINK

Sweet whites, rich reds, vintage port, malty ale, cider,
whisky.

David Jowett

KING STONE DAIRY

[Instagram icon] @davidjowett

[Twitter icon] @kingstonedairy

[web icon] www.kingstonedairy.com

KING STONE DAIRY

David Jowett's youth may belie his substantial experience, but the quality of his unique creations does not.

His eye was first turned towards cheese whilst working as a chef in his late teens. He left catering to work for leading cheesemonger Paxton and Whitfield, giving him a broad window on the world of international, as well as British, artisan cheese. A familiarisation trip to Ram Hall, creator of one of the country's leading sheep's cheeses, Berkswell, further fanned the flame of his ambitions and he decided upon a career as cheesemaker. He took up an internship at Ram Hall before embarking on The School of Artisan Food's Advanced Diploma, then the country's most advanced cheesemaking qualification. Lessons learned under the equally talented Val Bines and Ivan Larcher while there propelled David towards spells at Neal's Yard Dairy, the US's Jasper Hill Dairy and two years as cheesemaker at Gorsehill Abbey.

At the ripe age of 25 he decided it was time to strike out on his own. In 2015 he formed a partnership with the Hayne family at King Stone Farm to transform its pasture, rich with herbage and native grasses, into Rollright, the first of his creations, named after the nearby Neolithic stones. A spruce-bound washed-rind with a nod to Vacherin, Rollright won followers at the highest levels from the first releases and has evolved to become a new British classic. In 2018 it was soon joined by Evenlode, a semi-soft washed-rind.

In 2019 the dairy moved to premises on Manor Farm in Chedworth, and the building of a new dairy and maturation area should see the cheeses develop a wider following, continually building on quality and variety due to David's ever-questing spirit.

ROLLRIGHT

STYLE

Soft ,Washed Rind

RENNET

Animal

MILK TYPE

Cow: Friesian,
Montbéliarde,
Shorthorn, Simmental

 280g, 1kg

 Disk

TASTING NOTE

A spruce-lined buttery creation possessing an even,
oozing core with savoury nut and herbal notes, and a
rind that's a course in itself: macadamia, crystallised
game and porcini. Exceptional.

WHERE TO BUY

National wholesalers and regional cheesemongers. See
website.

WHAT TO DRINK

Aromatic off-dry white, light red, medium cider or
malty ale.

EVENLODE

STYLE

Semi Soft, Washed
Rind

RENNET

Animal

MILK TYPE

Cow: Friesian,
Montbéliarde,
Shorthorn, Simmental

400g, 1kg

Disk

TASTING NOTE

A rich cheese with warm hay and floral notes over
chanterelle mushroom on the nose, and milled multi-
seed flavours clenched in a semi-firm palate of warmed
floral cream.

WHERE TO BUY

National wholesalers and regional cheesemongers. See
website.

WHAT TO DRINK

Semi-sweet white, mead, malty ale.

Steve, Frank and Archie Reynolds

KINGCOTT DAIRY

[Instagram] @kingcottdairy
[Twitter] @kingcottdairy
[web] www.kingcottdairy.co.uk

KINGCOTT DAIRY

◎   STAPLEHURST, KENT

Steve Reynolds came from a line of dairy farmers in Somerset, but a financial education and a two-decade career in insurance put a full stop to it.

In 1996, the appeal of corporate life fully exhausted, he returned to the land with wife Karen, starting a small milk-focused dairy herd in Kent. The Good Life it wasn't. The BSE crisis hit the same year, the fallout from which had barely abated before the ultra-low milk prices of the early 2000s meant that something had to be done or the herd would have to be sold. Karen took a cheesemaking course at Reaseheath College in Nantwich and, with the help of tutor Chris Ashby, developed the recipe for Kentish Blue. The decision didn't lead to an immediate turnaround of fortunes, as it takes time and money to develop a product and find a market for it, but in growing the cheese business organically they reached a position where the farm could survive with its relatively small herd and employ a next generation.

In 2014, with elder son Frank on board, the Reynolds began shifting the herd away from Holstein Friesians and towards milk more suitable for high-grade cheesemaking. They introduced the feisty-sounding though placid Viking Reds into the herd, the breed renowned for yielding a smaller volume of solid-rich milk. The resulting cheese has consequently benefitted, being richer and more flavoursome. Frank has also added a new cheese to the range. Blue is still the colour but the style is softer, closer to a Gorgonzola, providing a complementary partner to Karen's more robust Stilton style. It seems you can take the family out of dairy farming, but only for so long. The City's loss is Kent's great gain.

KENTISH BLUE

 AGE AT RELEASE

8 weeks

STYLE

Semi Hard, Blue

RENNET

Vegetarian

MILK TYPE

Cow: Viking Red,
Holstein Friesian

 2.5kg

Drum

TASTING NOTE

The core, enjoyed first, gives a creamy paste with
flavours of porcini broth threaded with an even,
piquant, blue veining. The rind is more darkly
flavoured, with red game and high-tone earthy
penicillin notes.

WHERE TO BUY

Via website or wholesalers and cheesemongers
countrywide. See web for details.

WHAT TO DRINK

Sweet whites, port, winter ale, medium cider.

KINGCOTT BLUE

AGE AT RELEASE

7 weeks

STYLE

Semi Soft, Blue

RENNET

Vegetarian

MILK TYPE

Cow: Viking Red,
Holstein Friesian

 1kg

Ammonite

TASTING NOTE

A gentle blue with full cream to the fore, giving notes
of dried pear, quince and hints of forest floor.

WHERE TO BUY

Via website or wholesalers and cheesemongers
countrywide. See web for details.

WHAT TO DRINK

Sweet whites, tawny port, medium cider.

Jodie Scheckter

LAVERSTOKE
PARK FARM

:camera: @laverstoke

:bird: @laverstoke

:calendar: www.laverstoke.co.uk

LAVERSTOKE
PARK FARM

⊙ OVERTON, HAMPSHIRE

───────────────

It takes an uncompromising spirit to extract the best from any endeavour, so when an ex-Formula One champion sets out to make cheese, it's unlikely to be second rate.

Jodie Scheckter's career following his 1979 championship win with Ferrari saw him both as commentator and entrepreneur, which allowed him in 1996 to purchase 2,500 acres of farmland at the southern tip of the North Wessex Downs near Overton. A stated desire to produce the best-tasting, healthiest food for his family became rather more with a visit to a buffalo herd. Contrary to prevailing wisdom in the dairy business, he was attracted by the breed's low yields, believing it directly contributed to quality. The yields, less than one third of most dairy breeds, result in to higher levels of butterfats and proteins, and, when handled well, to increased flavours in cheese.

Thought to have been introduced to the Mediterranean from China in the 1600s, the Asian Water Buffalo is a regular sight in many parts of Italy, particularly the south, where the mozzarella tradition began. An pure-breed, hardy animal, it adapts well to new environments and has fewer health problems. Its easy nature made it a natural milking animal, and its low-yields to high-solid ratio favoured cheese.

In 2003 Jodie purchased a herd of 200 buffalo from Bob Palmer, a Warwickshire cheesemaker. Bob helped Jodie to develop Laverstoke's mozzarella before its release in 2005. Mozzarella is a 'pasta filata' (spun paste) cheese. The curds are set and cut before being steeped in hot water or whey and then kneaded until an elastic, stringy texture is obtained. The finest is firmer and more flavourful than much encountered in the UK, as it is best consumed within days of manufacture, a factor that encouraged Jodie to predict there would be a strong home market for his unique product. A Gouda and Cheddar have been added to the range, as well as ice cream, all from the herd's milk.

The health of his farm is paramount and operations are run to organic and biodynamic principles, owing to a belief that to compromise would diminish soil diversity and sustainability, and in turn consumer wellbeing.

MOZZARELLA

 AGE AT RELEASE

3 days

STYLE

Fresh

RENNET

Vegetarian

MILK TYPE

Buffalo

 125g

 Ball

TASTING NOTE

Firm textured and delicate with clean, floral notes and hints of rice pudding.

WHERE TO BUY

Wholesalers and cheesemongers countrywide. See web for details.

WHAT TO DRINK

Sparkling, crisp whites, chilled reds, lager, dry cider.

Jo Clarke

LEICESTERSHIRE HANDMADE CHEESE COMPANY

⊙ @leicestershire_handmade_cheese

🐦 @sparkenhoefarm

🗂 www.leicestershirecheese.co.uk

LEICESTERSHIRE HANDMADE CHEESE COMPANY

⊙ UPTON, WARWICKSHIRE

In terms of quality, the style of a cheese, for instance Cheddar, Cheshire or Red Leicester, often doesn't mean much in the UK. In most cases the names for the territorial styles have been appropriated by large companies producing commercial bulk cheese. So, when Jo and David Clarke settled on calling their Sparkenhoe cheese a Red Leicester, it was with some trepidation. No unpasteurised farmhouse Red Leicester had been made since 1956, and for the cheese lover the name only conjured thought of pseudo-Cheddar with a fake tan.

As with many producers, low milk prices set the pair searching for alternative ways to make money from their farm. Yoghurt, milkshakes and even selling their third-generation dairy farm and herd of award-winning pedigree Holstein Friesians were all on the table, but it was an encounter with a friend who reminisced about pre-war Red Leicester that sent them on a cheesemaking course at Reaseheath in Nantwich. The couple dug out a recipe used on their Sparkenhoe Farm between 1745 and 1875 and set about re-creating the classic. To be successful they realised they would need to put as much distance as possible between their cheese and the ubiquitous orange blocks lining supermarket shelves, and it would demand no compromise.

Sparkenhoe Red Leicester is made from raw milk and traditionally crafted by a passionate and knowledgeable team who are hands-on from milking to maturation. Annatto (the orange colouring derived from the seeds of the achiote tree) is first added to the milk. The rennet follows and then the curd cut to grain-sized pieces, whey drained, and curd again cut into blocks and stacked. The blocks are then milled, salted, moulded and then pressed for 24 hours before being cloth-bound. The process, known as Cheddaring, the same used for making traditional Cheddar, might just as well be termed Red Leicestering as it is also native to this style. 2005 saw their first cheeses launched on the market, and the reviews and accolades that followed quickly reassured them the choice of name was justified.

Leicestershire Handmade Cheeses has added other creations to their offering, one of these the brainchild of Jo and David's son and fourth generation at the farm, William. Sparkenhoe Blue is similar in style to Stilton but unpasteurised and therefore unable to use the name despite being in one of the permitted counties. Blue Leicester might appropriately be a term that one day encapsulates the resurrected style. Then again, what's in a name?

SPARKENHOE BLUE

 AGE AT RELEASE

6 months

STYLE

Semi Hard, Blue

RENNET

Animal

MILK TYPE

Cow: Holstein Friesian

 6.8kg

 Cylinder

TASTING NOTE

The evenly distributed veining adds spice-rack diversity rather than bite to the sautéed chanterelle, butter and toffee biscuit flavours. A perfectly balanced myriad of forest floor notes adds to the experience an extra dimension.

WHERE TO BUY

Farm shop, via website or wholesalers and cheesemongers countrywide. See web for details.

WHAT TO DRINK

Rich reds, port, sweet whites and medium cider.

SPARKENHOE

AGE AT RELEASE

8 months

STYLE

Hard

RENNET

Animal

MILK TYPE

Cow: Holstein Friesian

10kg

Drum

TASTING NOTE

Sweet cream and carrot soup on the nose with a hint of caramel. Joined on the palate by dried autumn fruit, field mushroom and a citric tang on the finish. Outstanding.

WHERE TO BUY

Farm shop, via website or wholesalers and cheesemongers countrywide. See web for details.

WHAT TO DRINK

Mid-bodied reds, semi-sweet whites, malty beer or off-dry cider.

SPARKENHOE VINTAGE

AGE AT RELEASE

18 months

STYLE

Hard

RENNET

Animal

MILK TYPE

Cow: Holstein Friesian

10kg

Drum

TASTING NOTE

A powerful parcel of sweetness: carrot cake, caramel, nutmeg and buttered toast from the core, while the rind lends a orchard-box full of sun-dried apple, fig and sun-dried fungi. Exceptional.

WHERE TO BUY

Farm shop, via website or wholesalers and cheesemongers countrywide. See web for details.

WHAT TO DRINK

Full-bodied reds, tawny ports, sweet whites, malty beer or off-dry cider.

Simon Jones and Richard Tagg

LINCOLNSHIRE
POACHER

@poachercheese

@poachercheese

www.lincolnshirepoachercheese.com

LINCOLNSHIRE POACHER CHEESE

◎ ALFORD, LINCOLNSHIRE

Named after a folk song celebrating the joys of liberating a hare from under a gamekeeper's nose, the recipe for Lincolnshire Poacher was inspired by West Country Cheddar when in 1992 Simon Jones, fourth generation custodian of Ulceby Grange Farm, decided to add cheesemaking to the farm's output.

With the help of pioneering organic cheesemaker Dougal Campbell, Simon developed a cheese that was a Cheddar in process but with an Alpine influence, its gently elastic texture being a hallmark of the cheese today. It proved so popular locally that it had to be rationed periodically while Simon scaled up. In 1995 Richard Tagg took over cheesemaking duties, allowing Simon to focus on the farm, and Richard remains in control of the vat today. Simon's brother, Tim, returned from a career in London to assist development in 2000, providing a strong triumvirate that has helped turn all the milk from their 230 contented Holstein Friesians into a range of unique cheeses.

Ulceby Farm is set on the rolling chalk hills of the Lincolnshire Wolds overlooking fenland and, to the east, the quiet sentinels spinning their energy in the North Sea. The turbines might have been inspiration for the farm, as it is a net exporter of electricity, an ethos for sustainability having inspired the brothers to install solar panels, a wind turbine, straw pellet boiler and ground heat source pump to power the farm's activities.

They are also keen promoters of wildlife, using minimal chemicals on the soil and adopting a loose-control management of hedgerows, leaving longer periods of growth between cuttings to allow fauna time to settle. This approach goes beyond sympathetic agriculture, it manifestly benefits the cheese, as the more diverse the microflora is on the soil, the greater will be its presence in the milk and hence in the unpasteurised cheese, the proof of which can be tasted after the cheeses have spent their sixteen or more months maturing on cool pine shelves.

The origins of the cheese could be said to trace back beyond its inception in 1992, in that Jenny, the Jones boys' mother, was a Cordon Bleu chef and instilled in the pair an appreciation of taste and a love of quality.

LINCOLNSHIRE POACHER RED

AGE AT RELEASE

9 months

STYLE

Hard

RENNET

Vegetarian

MILK TYPE

Cow: Holstein
Friesian, Ayrshire

 10kg

 Drum

TASTING NOTE

Softer than the Lincolnshire Poacher, with a nose of roasted seeds, field mushroom and dried orchard fruit, followed by a palate that gives caramelised flavours of parsnip, cream and pepper, becoming minerally towards the rind. Outstanding.

WHERE TO BUY

Via website or wholesalers and cheesemongers countrywide. See web for details.

WHAT TO DRINK

Sweet whites, rich reds, tawny port, malty ale, strong cider.

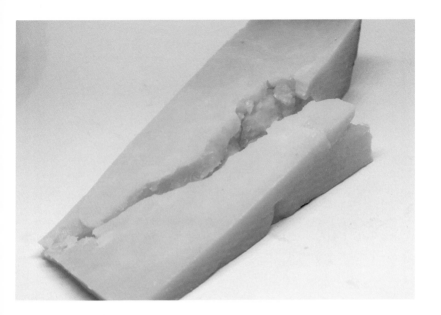

LINCOLNSHIRE POACHER

AGE AT RELEASE

16 months

STYLE

Hard

RENNET

Animal

MILK TYPE

Cow: Holstein
Friesian, Ayrshire

 20kg

 Large Drum

TASTING NOTE

The cheese bows then breaks with a reassuring
crumble, the rich paste yielding aromas of cashew,
custard and ripe mushroom. Flavours of seared white
game and hazelnut fill the palate before finishing with
a citric bite. Outstanding.

WHERE TO BUY

Via website or wholesalers and cheesemongers
countrywide. See web for details.

WHAT TO DRINK

Sweet whites, rich reds, tawny port, malty ale, strong
cider.

LOCH ARTHUR CAMPHILL COMMUNITY

It would be forgivable for the non-turophile (cheese lover) to overlook the importance of cheesemaking at the Loch Arthur Camphill Community, as it is only a part of a remarkable story.

One of a now-worldwide network of residential working communities started on the outskirts of Aberdeen by Austrian pediatrician Karl Konig in 1940, Loch Arthur provides support, education and employment for eighty people with learning disabilities. The 500-acre farm, nestled beside a small loch in the rolling Galloway hills, was acquired by the Community in 1984 and began churning butter from the milk of its two Jersey and two Ayrshire cows, in part to suit the skills of a resident with limited mobility but strong arms.

Cheese and yoghurt followed in a small way, but it wasn't until a year later, when Barry Graham joined as a volunteer and began exploring the area's historical farmhouse cheese culture, that one of the cornerstones of the revival of British cheese was set in place. Finding it had dwindled to virtually nothing, he sought to rekindle the tradition and make examples that tasted of their place by following the biodynamic principles upon which the Camp Hill communities are founded, and by using raw milk and traditional methods.

He quickly met others at the vanguard of the push for raw milk cheese, such as Humphrey Errington, James Aldridge and Randolph Hodgson, who assisted him in his task. He became a founder member of the Specialist Cheese Makers Association and a leading advocate for artisan cheese, and what began as a temporary role at the community turned into a lifelong cheese quest, one that has inspired many others.

Barry's passion goes beyond cheese though. He has helped to steer the community to its current position as one of the largest in the UK, encompassing a butchery, a bakery and a sizeable vegetable garden as well as non-food activities such as weaving and woodwork, all of which find outlet in the community's spectacular new farm shop and café. These have become popular tourist destinations, even for those not aware of Loch Arthur's now classic cheeses.

KILLYWHAN

AGE AT RELEASE

3 months

STYLE

Hard

RENNET

Vegetarian

MILK TYPE

Cow: Shorthorn, Meuse-Rhine-Issel, Fleckvieh

1.2kg

Drum

TASTING NOTE

The semi-firm core gives flavours of dried mushroom and cream that strengthen to earth and mineral at the rind.

WHERE TO BUY

Via the website or wholesalers and cheesemongers countrywide. See web for details.

WHAT TO DRINK

Semi-sweet white, medium-bodied reds, off-dry cider, malty ale.

FARMHOUSE

AGE AT RELEASE

7 months

STYLE

Hard

RENNET

Vegetarian

MILK TYPE

Cow: Shorthorn, Meuse-Rhine-Issel, Fleckvieh

8 kg

Drum

TASTING NOTE

A mild Cheddar with light game and mushroom notes.

WHERE TO BUY

Via the website or wholesalers and cheesemongers countrywide. See web for details.

WHAT TO DRINK

Medium-bodied reds, tawny ports, sweet whites, malty beer or off-dry cider.

MATURE FARMHOUSE

AGE AT RELEASE

12 months

STYLE

Hard

RENNET

Vegetarian

MILK TYPE

Cow: Shorthorn, Meuse-Rhine-Issel, Fleckvieh

8kg

Drum

TASTING NOTE

A robust Cheddar with dusty nut and pepper notes on the nose and palate with a spice kick.

WHERE TO BUY

Via the website or wholesalers and cheesemongers countrywide. See web for details.

WHAT TO DRINK

Medium-bodied reds, tawny port, sweet whites, malty beer or off-dry cider.

Mike Smales

LYBURN FARM

⊙ @lyburncheese

𝕏 @lyburncheese

▭ www.lyburnfarm.co.uk

LYBURN FARM

A New Forest institution, the Smales family began coaxing flavour from its soil in 1952.

The father of current owner Mike Smales started milking at Little Buckholt Farm, West Tytherley with just three Guernsey cows. Seventeen years later Mike's father brought the family a little south to Lyburn Farm, a tranquil but run-down set of buildings with 270 acres, straddling the river Blackwater at the northern edge of the forest. He invested in a dairy unit and began milking 200 cows, then a sizable herd. In the years that followed, the family diversified into organic vegetables, and in particular pumpkins and squash. However, this wasn't enough to compensate for dwindling milk prices, and in 1999 Mike sought further safeguards by turning some of their milk into cheese.

Whilst cheese had been produced by the Cistercians at Beaulieu, and there had been a little farmhouse output in the area subsequently, the New Forest had no great tradition of cheesemaking. Mike had free reign to come up with something that would become synonymous with Lyburn, rather than adhere to any regional expectation. A fan of gouda styles, he developed washed curd recipes (where whey is released from the vat and replaced with hot water, assisting the curd to shed more whey and develop sweeter characters). The dairy now produces 300 wheels week, which are graded at eight weeks old to determine what age they will be matured to. As they age they change, from gouda to Cheddar to parmesan in character.

Lyburn Gold is the youngest incarnation, released at 3 months, Winchester at 9 months, and Old Winchester the eldest at 18 months or more and robust like a fine parmesan or Old Amsterdam. Lyburn Farm now processes half the milk of its cows to produce these, as well as Stoney Cross, a Tomme de Savoie style, and a few joint ventures, bringing the number of cheeses in the pristine maturing rooms to around 10,000 at any one time.

The cheeses have an enviable reputation for consistency, a medal tally that would shame a general and a wide range of outlets from cruise liners collecting from the nearby port of Southampton, to the exceptionally successful Hampshire Farmer's Markets, which Mike was instrumental in setting up twenty years ago. Mike's son, Jonathan, is now the third generation at Lyburn, managing the herd, one of a team of over twenty-strong working on the farm, many of whom work with the vegetables. The pumpkins are still a popular seasonal item to bolster turnover, ensuring that, unlike much farmhouse production, their peak is not just Christmas but Halloween too.

STONEY CROSS

 AGE AT RELEASE

2 months

STYLE

Semi Hard

RENNET

Vegetarian

MILK TYPE

Cow: Holstein
Friesian

 3kg

Drum

TASTING NOTE

A lovely chamois-leather feel to the rind on the palate with wild mushroom and mineral notes and a core that gives flavours of fresh mushroom broth and earth.

WHERE TO BUY

Wholesalers and cheesemongers countrywide. See web for details.

WHAT TO DRINK

Aromatic off-dry whites, medium-bodied reds, cider and hoppy ales.

LYBURN GOLD

 AGE AT RELEASE

3 months

STYLE

Hard

RENNET

Vegetarian

MILK TYPE

Cow: Holstein
Friesian

 5.5kg

 Drum

TASTING NOTE

Sweet crème caramel and butter notes dominate the
core on the nose and the palate gives an elastic crunch
yielding semi-strong hazelnut and warm butter notes.

WHERE TO BUY

Wholesalers and cheesemongers countrywide. See web
for details.

WHAT TO DRINK

Medium to rich reds, sweet whites, tawny port, malty
beer, cider.

WINCHESTER MATURE

 AGE AT RELEASE

9 months

STYLE

Hard

RENNET

Vegetarian

MILK TYPE

Cow: Holstein
Friesian

 4.5kg

 Drum

TASTING NOTE

Semi-rich sugared nuts on the nose with a brittle palate
giving dried orchard fruit, chanterelle mushroom and
subtle caramel notes.

WHERE TO BUY

Wholesalers and cheesemongers countrywide. See web
for details.

WHAT TO DRINK

Medium to rich reds, sweet whites, tawny port, malty
beer, cider.

OLD WINCHESTER

AGE AT RELEASE

18 months

STYLE

Hard

RENNET

Vegetarian

MILK TYPE

Cow: Holstein
Friesian

 4.5kg

 Drum

TASTING NOTE

Rich peanut brittle, dried apple and hazelnut notes
notes on the nose and a rich crystal-crunch on the
palate with notes of toffee apple, spice and dried cep.
Outstanding.

WHERE TO BUY

Wholesalers and cheesemongers countrywide. See web
for details.

WHAT TO DRINK

Rich reds, port, sweet whites, malty beer, sweet cider.

Catherine Mead

LYNHER DAIRIES

⊙ @cornish.yarg
𝕏 @cornishyarg
▭ www.lynherdairies.co.uk

LYNHER DAIRIES

———————————

There are few single-producer cheeses in Britain as easily recognisable or well-known as Cornish Yarg. Its name, and the reason for it, has entered the lexicon of quiz-goers countrywide. This is due as much to its original creators as it is to the efforts of Catherine Mead, who since 1995 has helped guide it into the hearts of the nation.

In 1984 Alan and Jenny Gray, farmers on Bodmin Moor, came across a recipe in their attic for nettle-wrapped cheese written in 1615. They revived the style, understood to date back to the 13th century, and in their search for a name settled on their surname spelled backwards. The regionally-sounding Yarg was thought far more appealing than the dubious Gray Cheese.

It was still relatively unknown when they sold the recipe to Mike and Margaret Horrell, farmers on the Duchy of Cornwall Estate. In 1995 the Horrells sought advice from Catherine Mead, a dairy business consultant who had recently returned to her family's farm in Pengreep, near Ponsanooth. A joint venture was born that saw production quickly taken to capacity on the Horrell's farm, then spread to Catherine's also. The cheese was produced on both sites until Catherine took over when the Horrells retired in 2006.

Cornish Yarg is based on a Caerphilly recipe. The make is cooler than that for Cheddar, retaining more moisture, but the process is similar in that the curds, once cut and drained, are cut into blocks and allowed to drain some more before being milled, moulded and pressed. The cheeses are then brined before receiving their covering of nettles.

Nettles, a native of hedgerows and forest edges, thrive only in precise climatic conditions and have so far thwarted attempts at cultivation. Thus the 1.5 tonnes of Cornish Yarg made a week require covering in foraged leaves, a task employing upwards of twenty people between May and July. The leaves are dipped in citric acid (to prevent browning) and frozen, then thawed to order. The leaves help to raise the pH on the rind, assisting breakdown and development of the trademark white mould dusting. Garlic Yarg has joined the classic, the cheese identical until maturation when the mould-inhibiting Allium ursinum leaves, again foraged from local woodlands, are applied, helping to produce a crumblier cheese with a gentle garlic hint.

In 2017 the dairy grew once again to accommodate a new gouda-Alpine hybrid. Kern, a wax coated, washed-curd cheese made with Alpine starters, is unique in looks and taste. With a name meaning 'round' in Cornish, as well as the first syllable of Kernow (the Cornish for Cornwall), it will no doubt soon become as synonymous with its county of birth as its leaf-clad siblings.

GARLIC YARG

AGE AT RELEASE

5 weeks

STYLE

Hard

RENNET

Vegetarian

MILK TYPE

Cow

1kg, 1.7kg, 4kg

Drum

TASTING NOTE

A clean, crumbly cheese with fresh curd notes threaded with lemon aromas beneath an easy garlic influence.

WHERE TO BUY

Via the website or wholesalers and cheesemongers countrywide. See web for details.

WHAT TO DRINK

Aromatic off-dry whites, light chilled reds, cider and hoppy ales.

CORNISH YARG

 AGE AT RELEASE

5 weeks

STYLE

Hard

RENNET

Vegetarian

MILK TYPE

Cow

 1kg, 1.7kg, 4kg

Drum

TASTING NOTE

A semi-complex cheese with notes of single cream, field mushroom and fresh grass on the nose, following through on the palate with a citric and nettle-herb note.

WHERE TO BUY

Via the website or wholesalers and cheesemongers countrywide. See web for details.

WHAT TO DRINK

Aromatic off-dry whites, light chilled reds, cider and hoppy ales.

STITHIANS

AGE AT RELEASE
8 months

STYLE
Hard

RENNET
Animal

MILK TYPE
Cow

1kg, 1.7kg, 4kg

Drum

TASTING NOTE

An even, dry-textured cheese with core flavours of crème de cacao, spice and custard, leading to a rind with dry-stone mineral notes. Outstanding.

WHERE TO BUY

Via the website or wholesalers and cheesemongers countrywide. See web for details.

WHAT TO DRINK

Semi-sweet whites, medium-bodied reds, malty ales, off-dry cider.

KERN

 AGE AT RELEASE

14 months

STYLE

Hard

RENNET

Animal

MILK TYPE

Cow

 1kg, 1.7kg, 4kg

Drum

TASTING NOTE

A richy textured crack-crumble core with sweet peanut, toffee and dried fruit notes and a palate that works into a pudding-paste. Outstanding.

WHERE TO BUY

Via the website or wholesalers and cheesemongers countrywide. See web for details.

WHAT TO DRINK

Semi-sweet whites, fruity reds, malty ale and off-dry cider.

Lawrence and Karen Wright

MIDDLE CAMPSCOTT
FARM

◎ @middlecampscott

▭ www.middlecampscott.co.uk

MIDDLE CAMPSCOTT FARM

A distant holiday memory has inspired nearly three decades of cheese production at Middle Campscott Farm.

As a child, Lawrence Wright once spent a fortnight on a rambling farm on a hill above the town of Lee on the North Devon coast. Despite the rain, a slippery yard and terrifyingly large cows, it drew him back in his forties after a change in government legislation left his family's architecture business without a client. He and wife Karen, also an architect, had wanted to move the family out of London for some time, so when they saw the farm for sale in 1992 they swapped pencils for pens.

They developed a small flock of Friesland sheep and, after attending a cheesemaking course with author and consultant Rita Ash, started making a hard-pressed cheese with a relatively early release that would allow further ageing, something that would help in a market then unknown. It proved popular, which they attributed to rich grasses and diverse herbage benefiting from the proximity to the Bristol Channel. The site's mild climate also permitted year-round grazing for a small herd of Ruby Devon cattle, contributing to organic pasture management.   Cheese was only to be a part of the business; beef and lamb, as well as milk, yoghurt, fleeces, knitting wool, kits, woven blankets and throws would also provide year-round income.

Over time the Wrights sought diversity in their flock, moving away from exclusively Friesland sheep. The animals were good for milk volume but less of a meat or wool breed of choice. A desire to understand how the milk of traditionally 'non-dairy' breeds could adapt to cheesemaking was also a factor. Initially they brought in Zwartbles, a dual-purpose breed, close to the Frieslands, also originating in Holland, their dark coats adding to variety in the wool. Shetlands followed, small but milky with fine textured, colored wool. The couple found an inverse correlation between quality and volume. The 'non-dairy' breeds yielded lower volumes but gave milk richer in solids and flavour.

Over the years methods on the farm have adapted to facilitate cheesemaking within the constraints of a heavily committed daily work schedule. Once milking took place twice a day but now only the morning milk is taken for cheesemaking, the lambs left with their mothers during the day and taken off overnight. It's a balance that allows lambs to be with their mothers until weaning, and though milk is lost for cheese, value is transferred to the lamb. It's a practice that others in the cheese world are exploring at a time when many consumers are demanding that their food producers look to more compassionate methods of animal husbandry.

MIDDLE CAMPSCOTT

AGE AT RELEASE

3 months

STYLE

Hard

RENNET

Vegetarian

MILK TYPE

Sheep

2kg

Drum

TASTING NOTE

Dry and crumbly. Hot walnut, earth and game nose with a piquant palate of trompette de la mort, dried venison and cedar.

WHERE TO BUY

Via the website or retailers and farmers' markets locally. See web for details.

WHAT TO DRINK

Rich reds, tawny port, sweet whites, rich ale and sweet cider.

Jamie Montgomery

MONTGOMERY CHEESE

🖥 www.montgomerycheese.co.uk

MONTGOMERY CHEESE

The herd at Manor Farm grazes rich Somerset pasture, part of which overlaps the slopes of the former Neolithic settlement on Cadbury Hill, home to forts through the ages including, legend has it, King Arthur's court of Camelot.

The fort mentality continues to this day at the farm. One of only a handful producing traditionally Cheddared, unpasteurised, cloth-bound Cheddar, Montgomery's was once a near-lone survivor against the onslaught of mass-produced incarnations, a thread that has kept the tradition alive and allowed others to taste the potential of true Cheddar.

Jamie Montgomery, currently setting the curd, is the third generation to make cheese, following mother Elizabeth and grandfather Sir Archibald Langman, who bought the farm in 1911. From beginnings among over 400 farmhouse cheesemakers, by the end of World War Two their brethren had dwindled to a handful. Elizabeth remained resolute in using traditional methods despite strong overtures from the Milk Marketing Board to pasteurise and modernise. She knew that, were she to follow their guidance, quality would be loser. The cause was advanced by Jamie as he took over during the 1980s and he has since built upon the farm's reputation with a passion for his subject that sees no avenue unexplored for improvement in his cheeses.

Whilst sharing a friable, crystalline nature, occasionally prone to bluing along fissures, the cheeses' flavours change from batch to batch depending upon a variety of factors. The day of week will influence the character of the make depending upon which of the traditional 'pint-pot' starters is used (the traditional Cheddar cultures saved for the industry by Barber's). As with any cultures, their rotation is paramount for healthy cheesemaking. The weather and grass moisture play a role, as does the herbage mixture in the pastures being grazed. The consistent element is quality, and, when asked the secret to Montgomery Cheddar's excellence, Jamie replies that there is no one factor and all improvements are the result of tweaks to discover their impact overall. True to his philosophy, he is approaching a change of herd in the same way. Once shorthorn, then Ayrshire, the herd is now Friesian, though a slow change of breeding back to Ayrshire is underway.

The farm also has a small herd of Jersey cows. Their milk is responsible for Ogleshield, a West Country version of Raclette with a semi-soft core and a gently pungent, brine-washed rind. It's a delightful and welcome interloper that breached the ramparts in the early 2000s.

CHEDDAR

AGE AT RELEASE

11 months

STYLE

Hard

RENNET

Animal

MILK TYPE

Cow: Ayrshire x
Friesian

 24kg

 Large Drum

TASTING NOTE

A wonderfully mottled, lived-in, rind gives aromas of
warm forest floor and dry loft-apple, and the cream-
crunch core has a solid bite with notes of hazelnut,
crème caramel and milled seed, with yeasty, marmite
undertones. Exceptional.

WHERE TO BUY

Via the website or wholesalers and cheesemongers
countrywide. See web for details.

WHAT TO DRINK

Sweet whites, rich reds, vintage port, malty ale, cider,
whisky.

Graham Kirkham

MRS KIRKHAM'S CHEESE

 @mrs-kirkhams-lancashire-cheese

@mrskirkhamslanc

www.mrskirkhamscheese.co.uk

MRS KIRKHAM'S CHEESE

◎ GOOSNARGH, LANCASHIRE

To simply say that Mrs Kirkham's Lancashire is a rare gem of a cheese would be misleading. It's less than rare where only a single example remains.

One of the oldest territorials (cheeses named after the county or area they originated from), Lancashire can trace its roots back to the thirteenth century, but the effect of World War Two virtually eliminated the style. The 200 producers in 1939 were forced to stop during rationing and only a handful went back to making traditional Lancashire cheese afterwards, its slow and delicate two or three-day make not competitive when compared to commercial cheeses.

When Ruth Kirkham began making cheese at Beesley Farm in 1978 (inheriting her mother's equipment and starting with a recipe from a farm in Inglewhite) there were only eight other farms making traditional unpasteurised Lancashire. Ten years later, when Randolph Hodgson from Neal's Yard Dairy approached her for supply, hers was the last remaining. Having come under pressure from The Milk Marketing Board to pasteurise her cheese, she was considering retirement. Randolph told her he would sell all she could make. He also encouraged her to cloth-bind and butter the cheese instead of dipping it in wax. 'Buttering up' was the traditional method of encouraging a natural rind that allowed character from naturally occurring moulds to permeate the cheeses and promote greater local integrity.

In the early 2000s Graham Kirkham, Ruth's son, began assisting, taking the cheeses to market and helping to build the brand. In 2008 he took over full-time with partner Kellie Whitehead and they quickly sought to strengthen the business ready for the next millennium. A new dairy and maturation room were built, and the team expanded, all while maintaining traditional methods including the two-day recipe. As a nod to a time where a smallholding might produce only enough milk to make a cheese every second or third day, curd would be formed on the first and set aside. The next day's curd would be added, and the batch would be left for another day before further curd was combined, or milling and moulding began. This gives the cheese its characteristic marbled appearance and fluffy crumble. Graham and Kellie's team continue the precious and precarious tradition of unpasteurised, cloth-bound and buttered-up Lancashire cheesemaking.

LANCASHIRE

 AGE AT RELEASE
6 months

STYLE
Semi Hard

RENNET
Animal

MILK TYPE
Cow: Holstein
Friesian

 10kg. 25kg

 Drum

TASTING NOTE

Alabaster pale with a fragility that belies the richness
of aromatics: rice pudding, butter and chanterelle on
the nose turn to white game, mushroom broth and
citrus on a fluffly-crumble palate. Outstanding.

WHERE TO BUY

Via website or wholesalers and cheesemongers
countrywide. See web for details.

WHAT TO DRINK

Aromatic off-dry whites, light chilled reds, cider and
hoppy ales.

Rose Grimond

NETTLEBED CREMERY

:camera: @nettlebedcheese

:bird: @nettlebedcheese

:calendar: www.nettlebedcreamery.com

NETTLEBED CREAMERY

📍 HENLEY-ON-THAMES, OXFORDSHIRE

Rose Grimond acknowledges the assistance of many in the formation of Nettlebed Creamery, from consultants to customers, as well as the inspiration given by the pioneers of the new wave in the 1980s: those who helped take artisan British cheese from a distant memory to something that could once again grace our plates. However, there would be little within her cheese to delight our palates without the considerable amount of mental energy she has expended on creating Nettlebed's range of new classics.

It was selling cheese from Orkney in Borough Market in the 2000s that flicked a switch for Rose, illuminating an idea to help diversify activities on her family's farm in Bix. The offerings of Borough Market having set the bar high, only examples to compete with the best would be good enough, and only cheeses that would reflect, and be in tune with, the environment at their source. After a year of trials and the construction of a spacious dairy with the provision for customer visits (a forward thinking but still rare consideration in cheese production), Nettlebed made its first cheese in January 2015. St Bartholomew, named after Nettlebed village church, is a nutty Alpine-influenced cheese. It was followed a year later by Bix, a triple cream drum. Highmoor and Witheridge are both newer additions to the range, following the talent of the first pair in their ability to distinguish themselves from other cheeses by sight alone, let alone complexity and particularity of taste.

The farm has been organic since 2000 and the cows live on fodder that includes clover, chicory, plantain and yarrow, all elements that influence complexity in the cheese. To enhance milk quality for cheesemaking, a programme of breeding Montbelliarde, Noweigan Red and Swiss Brown into the milk-focused Holstein Friesians has been adopted, a process that is already paying dividends on quality.

It proves that it is smart thinking that influences quality in cheese the most, as well as a desire to get it right, and at Nettlebed these factors have already allowed Rose and her team to carry the baton on from the pioneers.

Cow Breeds: Brown Swiss, Holstein Friesian, Montbéliarde, Norwegian Red

WITHERAGE

 **AGE AT RELEASE**

6 months

STYLE

Semi Hard

RENNET

Animal

 MILK TYPE

Cow: See text.

 2kg

Drum

TASTING NOTE

A rich core radiating aromas of sun-dried hay, caramel, cep mushroom and winged game, strengthening to the rind.

WHERE TO BUY

Wholesalers and cheesemongers countrywide. See website.

WHAT TO DRINK

Aromatic off-dry whites, light chilled reds, cider and hoppy ales.

BIX

 AGE AT RELEASE

2 weeks

STYLE

Soft, Bloomy

RENNET

Animal

MILK TYPE

Cow: See text.

 100g

 Button

TASTING NOTE

A triple cream recipe based on Chaource, with an even wrinkle to the rind, a basket of field mushrooms on the nose, and lemony citrus and cream poured over fresh hay on the palate.

WHERE TO BUY

Wholesalers and cheesemongers countrywide. See website.

WHAT TO DRINK

Sparkling, crisp white, dry cider or citric ale.

HIGHMOOR

AGE AT RELEASE

4 weeks

STYLE

Soft, Washed Rind

RENNET

Animal

MILK TYPE

Cow: See text.

 300g

 Tile

TASTING NOTE

A unique take on a Pavé d'Auge with a pungent cream, chanterelle and apricot nose, and a palate of crème brulée and alpine flowers. Outstanding.

WHERE TO BUY

Wholesalers and cheesemongers countrywide. See website.

WHAT TO DRINK

Aromatic off-dry white, light red, malty ale or medium cider.

Dave and Marilyn Johnson

NORSWORTHY

Dave Johnson, one-time naval engineer turned cow herdsman, took a step towards becoming one of the country's finest goat's cheesemakers when he babysat a herd in the late 1990s.

Such was he smitten that in 1999 he and wife Marilyn bought forty day-old kids and introduced them to their farm in the gentle hills between Exmoor and Dartmoor. Two years later they were supplying milk to local cheese and yoghurt producers as well as selling raw milk at farmers' markets. The herd grew and they found that, whilst surplus summer milk froze sufficiently well to feed the kids over winter, better value would be gained from creating their own cheese. The skills and dairy of Vera Tooke, a Dutch-born local cheesemaker, were employed and Norsworthy and Gunstone soon came into being, semi-soft and semi-hard washed-curd recipes inspired by Vera's homeland. Her retirement in 2006 prompted Dave and Marylin to build their own dairy and take the seamless step into making the cheeses themselves.

Goat's milk, one of the oldest dairy products, differs from cow's as it is closer to human milk, having smaller fat globules, making it easier to digest. It is also lower in lactose, making it a potential drinking choice for those with intolerance. However, these benefits matter little to anyone put off its cheese due to the goaty-musk taste often found if the milk is roughly handled, as it often is. The herd management, milking and cheesemaking at Norsworthy are all such a high standard that their cheeses express the milk's true potential. Dave and Marilyn choose not to pasteurise, believing it destroys bacteria and enzymes beneficial to flavour development.

Goats in the UK are often zero-grazed but theirs have access to pastures year round, further adding to the diversity of microflora in the milk that come through in the cheese. The rich array of flavours found in the cheeses are the result of expert navigation from soil to slice, a melding of careers.

Goat breeds: Alpine, Anglo Nubian, Saanen, Toggenberg

NORSWORTHY TILLERTON

 AGE AT RELEASE

10 days

STYLE

Soft, Bloomy

RENNET

Vegetarian

MILK TYPE

Goat: See notes for breeds.

 75g

 Button

TASTING NOTE

A fresh, clean goat's milk cheese with a lemony lactic centre with scents of fresh grass and parsley herb and a busy rind, full of goat-game and pepper notes.

WHERE TO BUY

See website for details.

WHAT TO DRINK

Sparkling, aromatic whites, light reds, hoppy ale and cider.

NORSWORTHY

AGE AT RELEASE

4 weeks

STYLE

Hard

RENNET

Vegetarian

MILK TYPE

Goat: See notes for breeds.

 2kg

Drum

TASTING NOTE

A characterful cheese with a complex broth of fresh mushroom and creamed rice at the core and clean earth and porcini at the rind.

WHERE TO BUY

See website for details.

WHAT TO DRINK

Aromatic off-dry whites, medium-bodied reds, cider and hoppy ales.

NORSWORTHY MATURE

AGE AT RELEASE

8 months

STYLE

Hard

RENNET

Vegetarian

MILK TYPE

Goat: See notes for breeds.

 2kg

Drum

TASTING NOTE

A richly flavoured cheese with an elastic break, giving sweet salted mixed nut and caramel from the core and a delicious rind with tobacco and crème brulée notes. Outstanding.

WHERE TO BUY

See website for details.

WHAT TO DRINK

Rich off-dry whites, chilled tawny port, malty ale.

Cheesemaker Martin Atkinson

NORTHUMBERLAND CHEESE COMPANY

@nlandcheese

@nlandcheese

www.northumberlandcheese.co.uk

NORTHUMBERLAND CHEESE COMPANY

◎ BLAGDON, NORTHUMBERLAND

The tranquil Rede Valley, foundation point for the Northumberland Cheese Company, has had a turbulent past. As rugged border country it was home to the Border Reivers (English and Scottish border raiders) who for four centuries evaded governance. Maybe it was a remnant of their spirit that prompted Marc Robertson, founder at Northumberland Cheese Company, to break free from the constraints of meat subsidies in 1984 and start to milk his sheep in the hope of extracting better value from his livestock. Before he embarked on cheesemaking however, he did a little raiding of his own, gathering inspiration for his business from gouda producers in the Netherlands.

Fresh from his travels, his first cheese was made in a bucket above the farmhouse sink and matured in the cellar of a local hotel. By his own admission it was not what he had in mind, but the experience sent him on a cheesemaking course at Reeseheath in Nantwich. After converting an 18th century outbuilding into a dairy he released his first cheese. Redesdale, a subtle young ewe's milk cheese still made by the dairy, was an instant hit with locals. In 1987 an encounter with a Dutch dairy farmer led Marc to experiment with purchased cow's milk and the company's signature cheese, Coquetdale, was first moulded. The dairy grew with the opportunities provided by an on-tap supply of cow's milk, and shepherding became untenable so the flock was sold.

The company now makes 11 cheeses. Cow's milk from the Blagdon Estate, where Marc moved the business to in 1996, is accountable for 95% of production, but goat's and sheep's milk are bought in, both from single herds. The cheeses are made to a gouda recipe (whereby the curd is 'scalded' with hot water prior to moulding to encourage whey release and the development of the signature sweet notes) that Marc adapted to suit his milk and his market.

Marc, now retired, retains an active interest in the company despite having sold it to Bradbury's, the historic Derbyshire wholesaler. Perhaps influenced by the occasional raid from Marc, albeit just for a slice of cheese and cup of tea, they have kept his cheeses true to their origins.

REIVER

STYLE

Hard

RENNET

Vegetarian

MILK TYPE

Cow: Holstein
Friesian

2.5kg

Drum

TASTING NOTE

The core gives flavours of sweet cream, warm hay and hints of caramel, while the rind adds an interesting mineral dimension of dried fungus and moss.

WHERE TO BUY

Via the website or wholesalers and cheesemongers countrywide. See web for details.

WHAT TO DRINK

Mid-bodied reds, semi-sweet whites, malty beer or off-dry cider.

COQUETDALE

AGE AT RELEASE

3 months

STYLE

Hard

RENNET

Vegetarian

MILK TYPE

Cow: Holstein
Friesian

2.5kg

Drum

TASTING NOTE

A lighter beast than Reiver, with pleasing brothy notes and a
saline tang to the core.

WHERE TO BUY

Via the website or wholesalers and cheesemongers
countrywide. See web for details.

WHAT TO DRINK

Light to mid-bodied reds, semi-sweet whites, best ale, off-dry
cider.

BRINKBURN

AGE AT RELEASE

3 months

STYLE

Hard

RENNET

Vegetarian

MILK TYPE

Goat

2.5kg

Drum

TASTING NOTE

A lovely cheese with high-tone floral and hay notes on the
creamy-citric paste and a high tone wild mushroom broth at the
rind. Outstanding.

WHERE TO BUY

Via the website or wholesalers and cheesemongers
countrywide. See web for details.

WHAT TO DRINK

Aromatic off-dry whites, light chilled reds, cider and hoppy ales.

Rachel Yarrow

NORTON AND YARROW

@nortonandyarrowcheese

@nortonandyarrow

www.nortonandyarrow.co.uk

NORTON AND YARROW

Although farming was in Rachel Yarrow and Fraser Norton's blood, courtesy of parents and grandparents respectively, it was never of a goat or dairy type. So, it was a bold idea in 2014, during a holiday in Sicily, that set them on course to tend goats and make cheese from their milk.

With Rachel still teaching English and Fraser working for an NGO, they bought a pair of goats and began cheesemaking trials over their kitchen sink at home. The process gave them confidence enough to buy milk in whilst developing their own pure-bred herd of Anglo Nubian goats on a farm owned by Earth Trust, an environmental learning charity. With advice from leading UK cheesemaking consultant Paul Thomas and the assistance of Rose Grimond at Nettlebed Creamery, they were able to sell their first cheese in 2016. Sinodun Hill, a lactic-set truncated pyramid, named after a hill overlooking the farm, won immediate acclaim, including best new cheese at the Artisan Cheese Awards in Melton Mowbray. Further awards followed as well as telephone calls from major wholesalers, all of whom have helped the couple tweak their recipe, now at a purpose built dairy at the farm.

Attention to detail and a questing spirit are hallmarks of their operation, as well as an understanding that a great cheese comes from great milk. To that end, they are keen to allow the milk's natural microflora and that of the environment to provide the narrative and they practice a policy of minimal intervention as far as ripening cultures, advanced skills for a company so young. Also, in choosing Anglo Nubian goats, the Jerseys of the goat world in that they produce rich milk, high in butterfats, and grazing them on wildflower meadows (and its high-grade hay in the winter) they wisely realised that much of their job as artisan cheesemakers would already be done. Apart, that is, from milking 60 goats twice a day, seven days a week, and making cheese in between.

Their cheese, as are many in this guide, is therefore fantastically good value when you consider the effort taken to make it.

BRIGHTWELL ASH

AGE AT RELEASE
1 week

STYLE
Fresh

RENNET
Animal

MILK TYPE
Goat: Anglo-Nubian

Small Round

TASTING NOTE

Fresh & clean. Floral milk on the nose. Pleasing fine-grain palate with notes of grape and candied fruit in floral cream. Rind a little richer with gentle straw and lichen notes. Outstanding.

WHERE TO BUY

National wholesalers and regional cheesemongers. See website.

WHAT TO DRINK

Sparkling wine, dry cider, chilled red.

SINODUN HILL

AGE AT RELEASE

2 weeks

STYLE

Fresh, Bloomy

RENNET

Vegetarian

MILK TYPE

Goat: Anglo-Nubian

200g

Truncated Pyramid

TASTING NOTE

The delicate rind emits scents of pressed meadow flowers, hazelnut and sweet goat milk, while the palate provides a myriad of floral notes threaded with lemon.

WHERE TO BUY

National wholesalers and regional cheesemongers. See website.

WHAT TO DRINK

Sparkling, crisp white, dry cider or citric ale.

Tali Eichner

PLAW HATCH

Faced with closure in the eighties due to falling milk prices, Plaw Hatch Farm sought to raise funds by offering shares to locals and became a charitable trust. Since then ownership has spread to over 700 food-minded folk, many of them contributing to the 6,000 visits a month the farm receives for its produce.

The thriving dairy is just partly responsible for the draw. Its cheeses, raw milk, kefir and yoghurt are sold alongside the salad, vegetables, beef, lamb, pork and poultry that comes from the now two-farm co-operative covering 800 acres in the Ashdown Forest.

Plaw (an ancient word for plough) Hatch has for over thirty years been run along the principles of biodynamic agriculture set out by Austrian philosopher Rudolf Steiner in 1924. Biodynamic methods have much in common with organic principles, in that they emphasise the use of natural fertilisers and treatments and exclude all chemicals, but biodynamism also considers the treatment of animals, crops and soil as a holistic system, with an emphasis on local production and distribution. The farm goes even further, nurturing the farm's young volunteers and workers, something that forms part of its mission statement: 'to provide a working farm environment which honours learning, teaching, and personal and community growth and development.' Many farms local and further afield have benefitted from the well-informed crop of agricultural engineers the farm has educated.

The cheeses are seldom seen beyond the local area but, whilst a loss to the broader public, this is of benefit to the farm, in that profits that would otherwise be spent on distribution are instead channelled into sustaining a diverse and societally enriching farm.

CHEDDAR

 AGE AT RELEASE

6 months

STYLE

Hard

RENNET

Animal

MILK TYPE

Cow: Meuse-Rhine-
Issel, Montbéliarde,
Swiss Red

11kg, 22kg

Drum, Large Drum

TASTING NOTE

A crunchy conduit of desiccated woodland fare: wild
mushroom and sun-warmed logs on the nose and a
palate of beech nut and cream with a hint of chilli.

WHERE TO BUY

Farm shop and cheesemongers locally. See website.

WHAT TO DRINK

Sweet whites, rich reds, tawny port, malty ale, strong
cider.

CRUMBLY

 AGE AT RELEASE

3 months

STYLE

Hard

RENNET

Animal

MILK TYPE

Cow: Meuse-Rhine-
Issel, Montbéliarde,
Swiss Red

11kg

Drum, Large Drum

TASTING NOTE

Fresh cream and citric notes from the loose-knit core
and a darker scent closer to the rind reminiscent of
earthy field mushroom.

WHERE TO BUY

Farm shop and cheesemongers locally. See website.

WHAT TO DRINK

Mid-bodied reds, semi-sweet whites, malty beer or
off-dry cider.

QUARRY HOUSE FARM

If you have heard of Cotherstone cheese outside of Teesdale it probably means you have purchased it at Neal's Yard Dairy in London, the main buyer of this rare find whose reputation was once equal to that of the other Dales cheeses.

As with Wensleydale, Swaledale and Coverdale, Cotherstone's origins can be traced to the Cistercians at Jervaulx who tamed the landscape with limestone walls to enclose their flocks of sheep. Following the passing of cheesemaking from monk to farmer after the dissolution of the monasteries, cow became the livestock of choice and before long the rugged hills of County Durham around Cotherstone bristled with farmhouse cheesemakers creating the region's trademark style of butter-crumble cheese, distinct from those of neighbouring Yorkshire.

The wars and farm consolidation had diminished the number of Cotherstone cheesemakers to a handful by the 1980s, when Joan Cross started making it on her family's smallholding. She had been faced with a dilemma. The Milk Marketing Board were insisting she install a bulk tank as they no longer wished to collect churns containing the milk of the family's 10 cows. Having learned to make cheese with her mother at the kitchen table, she instead turned to her grandmother's Cotherstone recipe and began crafting small quantities for the local market around Barnard Castle.

More buttery than Wensleydale, though still with the characteristic citric edge, the Cotherstone comes in two forms. From the dairy it is fresh and wax sealed, ready to be eaten after a couple of weeks. Neal's Yard takes a larger size at a week old and ripens it with a naked rind for a further three weeks at its facility in Bermondsey, developing a drier crumble with mould-influenced aromatics. Whether from the farm or via the wholesaler, the cheeses are only available in tiny quantities and are the sole responsibility of Joan as she's the last remaining producer of this style. Once she decides to hang up her apron it may well be that an entire territorial category will disappear.

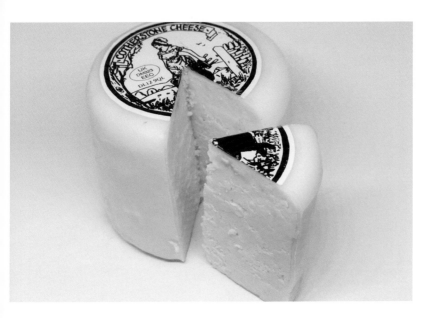

COTHERSTONE

 AGE AT RELEASE

4 weeks

STYLE

Semi Hard

RENNET

Vegetarian

MILK TYPE

Cow: Friesian

450g, 2.5kg

Small Drum, Drum

TASTING NOTE

Waxed: A richly flavoured cheese with a buttery crumble that breaks to a moreish paste full of sweet notes of white chocolate, rice pudding and light spice.

WHERE TO BUY

Neal's Yard dairy or from the farm.

WHAT TO DRINK

Aromatic off-dry whites, chilled fruity reds, cider and hoppy ales.

Mary Quicke

QUICKE'S

You might think that, having a connection to a farm dating back to 1540, there would be little left for a family to learn about their land.

Fourteen generations on, Mary Quicke is still thirsty for knowledge, and at a pace matched by few in the cheese world. A life-long surfer, trained writer, perennial gardener and seasoned arborist, she draws energy and experience from all she encounters to ensure her cheese business remains at the forefront of artisan practice as well as interacting positively with all it touches.

The cheese story at Quicke's dates from 1973 when Mary's parents, John and Prue, sought greater diversity on the farm due to arable surpluses. Bland, factory-produced Cheddar had become the staple post-war, so the couple chose to re-invigorate the near-extinct tradition of handmade, cloth-bound, long-matured Cheddar. They, as others, then had to sell their cheeses through the Milk Marketing Board, but by the late 70s a divergence of opinion led to a parting of ways. The Quickes wished their labour-intensive cheese to be sold on its value, but the MMB were only prepared to buy at the price they were offering, so the Quickes began to market their cheese directly instead. It was a success and others followed.

Mary, one of six siblings, was not the expected successor at the cheese vat. Part-way through a PhD in dramaturgy in London, while on a weekend back home, the cheese bug bit and she soon swapped the capital for the rippled greens of Devon to apprentice at a nearby farm. She then returned to assist her mother.

In 1987 Mary took over the running of the farm. Among the most valuable of her contributions to their cheesemaking progress has been the development and refinement of their herd of low-yielding hybrid cattle, the breeding of which is carefully controlled to ensure the best milk for their style of Cheddar. Another has been her deep-rooted understanding that the soil is where quality is made. The farm's 840 acres of pasture are grazed on a 24-hour rotation, the herd moving on every day to allow strong regrowth, thus encouraging deeper roots, more established plants and richer characters to find their way into the milk.

Quicke's is one of the larger artisan Cheddar producers, their uniquely mottled drums leaving Mary's 'cathedral of cheese' for markets around the globe. But quality here is not fettered by scale; when put into context, their annual output still equates to less a day's production at the largest commercial Cheddar factories.

GOAT

 AGE AT RELEASE

4-6 months

STYLE

Hard

RENNET

Vegetarian

MILK TYPE

Goat

27kg

Large Drum

TASTING NOTE

A clean cheese with persistent floral and citric undertones supporting rice pudding, nutmeg and meadow grass flavours. Outstanding.

WHERE TO BUY

Via the website or wholesalers and cheesemongers countrywide. See web for details.

WHAT TO DRINK

Off-dry sparkling, aromatic white, mid-bodied fruity red.

DEVONSHIRE RED

STYLE

Hard

RENNET

Animal / Vegetarian

MILK TYPE

Cow: See other cow
milk cheeses.

 27kg

 Large Drum

TASTING NOTE

A mild parcel of dried orchard fruit notes with vegetal
undertones.

WHERE TO BUY

Via the website or wholesalers and cheesemongers
countrywide. See web for details.

WHAT TO DRINK

Medium to rich reds, sweet whites, tawny ports, malty
beer, cider.

EXTRA MATURE

 AGE AT RELEASE

18 months

STYLE

Hard

RENNET

Animal / Vegetarian

MILK TYPE

Cow: Brown Swiss,
Holstein Friesian,
Jersey, Montbéliarde,
Swedish Red

 27kg

 Large Drum

TASTING NOTE

A semi-dry cheese with an easy crumble, yielding
milled seed and caramel notes on the nose. On the
palate a crystalline crunch softens to fine-grain
cream giving plentiful dried fruit, marmite and wild
mushroom aromas. Outstanding.

WHERE TO BUY

Via the website or wholesalers and cheesemongers
countrywide. See web for details.

WHAT TO DRINK

Rich reds, ports, sweet whites, malty beer, sweet cider.

VINTAGE

 AGE AT RELEASE

24 months

STYLE

Hard

RENNET

Animal / Vegetarian

MILK TYPE

Cow: Brown Swiss,
Holstein Friesian,
Jersey, Montbéliarde,
Swedish Red

 27kg

 Large Drum

TASTING NOTE

Rich butter and nut nose at the rind, with a lovely
crystalline crunch on the palate giving flavours of spice
yielding to aged butter, straw and dried cep.

WHERE TO BUY

Via the website or wholesalers and cheesemongers
countrywide. See web for details.

WHAT TO DRINK

Sweet whites, rich reds, vintage port, malty ale, cider,
whisky.

Mark Sharman and Debbie Mumford

SHARPHAM

- @sharpham_wine_and_cheese
- @sharphamwines
- www.sharpham.com

SHARPHAM

⊙ TOTNES, DEVON

Cheese and wine go together like fish and chips, but you are as likely to find a curd-stirring viticulturist as you are a potato-farming trawlerman. Distant cousins connected by fermentation, cheese and wine have little else in common in a business environment, which is why, when in the early eighties Maurice Ash sought to diversify on his 550-acre dairy farm, it was a bold move to start making both.

In 1961 Maurice had moved his Jersey dairy herd from Essex to the Sharpham Estate on the wooded slopes overlooking a bend on the River Dart two miles south of Totnes. An economist by training, by the late seventies he was aware that a move away from a commodity product was necessary if he was to sustain milking from a small breed. With a desire to create something unique to the UK, he travelled to France to learn how to make soft cheese, hitherto almost exclusively imported, and came back with a recipe for a Coulommiers Brie-style cheese. In 1981 a dairy was built in the 18th century coach yard and Sharpham Cheese was released, quickly creating a stir within the London restaurant scene due to its unique creamy texture and rich flavour, both hallmarks of Jersey milk.

The estate became a charitable trust in 1984, and the cheese and wine business a family partnership, now both run by Mark Sharman. Mark, nephew to Maurice, started on the wine side of the business but took over as MD in 1988. His partner Debbie Mumford became head cheesemaker in 1989, quickly expanding the range with the triple-cream Elmhirst and later the semi-hard Sharpham Rustic.

The dairy outgrew the coachyard in 2003 and is now partnered with the winery on a slope below the Sharpham Mansion. The Jersey herd is now farmed on the nearby Dartington Estate and goat milk is bought in for Ticklemore Goat as well as their unique mixed-milk cheeses, such as Sharpham Savour and Cremet, both of which can be claimed as British innovations.

Sharpham's cheeses are considered benchmarks for their styles. For the same management to be responsible for a vineyard producing over a dozen of the country's most respected wines, from 12,000 vines on the ideally situated south-facing slopes surrounding the dairy and winery, is truly remarkable.

SHARPHAM

 AGE AT RELEASE
2 weeks

STYLE
Soft, Bloomy

RENNET
Vegetarian

MILK TYPE
Cow: Jersey

 1kg

Small Disk

TASTING NOTE

The pleasingly thin rind gives way to sweetened cream and floral aromas with lemony notes to the core.

WHERE TO BUY

Via the website or wholesalers and cheesemongers countrywide. See web for details.

WHAT TO DRINK

Sparkling, chilled light red, dry white, cider.

ELMHIRST

STYLE
Soft, Bloomy

RENNET
Vegetarian

MILK TYPE
Cow: Jersey

 900g

 Square

TASTING NOTE

A complex cheese with ripe aromas of fresh cream, sautéed seed and flavours of seared chicken and chanterelle mushroom. Outstanding.

WHERE TO BUY

Via the website or wholesalers and cheesemongers countrywide. See web for details.

WHAT TO DRINK

Sparkling or white, light & fruity red.

TICKLEMORE GOAT

 AGE AT RELEASE

6 weeks

STYLE

Semi Hard

RENNET

Vegetarian

MILK TYPE

Goat

 450g, 1kg, 1.7kg

 Ammonite, Small Drum

TASTING NOTE

A mid-tone, clean goat musk underlies fresh straw and morel on the nose, while the palate gives rich field mushroom and white game flavours. Outstanding.

WHERE TO BUY

Via the website or wholesalers and cheesemongers countrywide. See web for details.

WHAT TO DRINK

Dry sparkling, aromatic white, mid-bodied fruity red.

RUSTIC

AGE AT RELEASE

8 weeks

STYLE

Semi Hard

RENNET

Vegetarian

MILK TYPE

Cow: Jersey

450g, 1kg, 1.7kg

Ammonite, Small
Drum

TASTING NOTE

A clean semi-crumbly core with gentle lactic notes
underlying cashew, cream and hay seed. Closer to the
rind are riper aromas turning to cep, pigeon breast and
stone mineral. Outstanding.

WHERE TO BUY

Via the website or wholesalers and cheesemongers
countrywide. See web for details.

WHAT TO DRINK

Off-dry sparkling, aromatic white, mid-bodied fruity
red.

Caroline Bell and Katie Matten

SHEPHERDS PURSE

- ⬡ @shepherdspurse
- 𝕏 @shepherdspurse
- ▭ www.shepherdspurse.co.uk

SHEPHERDS PURSE

Shepherds Purse was founded by farmer's wife Judy Bell in 1989 after she sought to discover whether she could help people suffering from cow's milk allergies by creating a cow's milk alternative from sheep milk on her family farm in North Yorkshire.

A pharmacist by training, at first Judy experimented with yoghurt and ice cream as well as cheese. However, it was the complexities of cheese making which sparked a passion in Judy, and that spark was then fuelled by the support of a local cheesemaker Les Lambert, from Kirkby Malzeard, who mentored Judy. With his guidance, after a year in her kitchen she moved the fledgling operation to a purpose-built micro-dairy where she created Olde York, a fresh ewe's milk cheese. With the encouragement of Les, Judy entered Nantwich International Cheese Awards in 1989, and when Olde York won a gold medal, it gave Judy the confidence to expand the range. A feta style cheese followed, as did further awards, increasing the demand. They began to experiment with blue cheese and in the mid-90s they added cow's milk to their range. In 1994 the first blue cheeses were launched, Yorkshire Blue Cows and Yorkshire Blue Ewes. In 1997 the sheep milk version was renamed Mrs Bell's Blue, and both Yorkshire Blue and Mrs Bell's Blue went on to win major international awards. In 2005 thanks to a local farmer they added a water buffalo milk blue cheese to the range.

In 1995 Judy was approached by one of the big supermarkets after Shepherds Purse won a major award at Nantwich. She agreed to supply, with the condition that she would be allowed to train their staff on speciality cheese and especially sheep milk cheese, which was unusual in the UK at the time. It is this approach to customer service that has helped Shepherds Purse to grow to become a company employing 35, now led by Judy's daughters Caroline Bell and Katie Matten.

YORKSHIRE BLUE

AGE AT RELEASE
8 weeks

STYLE
Semi Soft, Blue

RENNET
Vegetarian

MILK TYPE
Cow

1.4kg

Drum

TASTING NOTE
Pleasing buttery cheese filled with flavours of sweet cream, sautéed mushroom and a light blue spice.

WHERE TO BUY
Via the website or wholesalers and cheesemongers countrywide. See web for details.

WHAT TO DRINK
Rich reds, port, sweet whites and medium cider.

MRS BELL'S BLUE

AGE AT RELEASE
10 weeks

STYLE
Semi Soft, Blue

RENNET
Vegetarian

MILK TYPE
Sheep

1.4kg

Drum

TASTING NOTE
A mild Roquefort-blue tang threads the creamy flavours of macadamia and white game.

WHERE TO BUY
Via the website or wholesalers and cheesemongers countrywide. See web for details.

WHAT TO DRINK
Medium to rich reds, tawny port, sweet whites, medium cider.

HARROGATE BLUE

AGE AT RELEASE
10 weeks

STYLE
Semi Soft, Blue

RENNET
Vegetarian

MILK TYPE
Cow

1.4kg

Drum

TASTING NOTE
A striking and moreish parcel of gentle blue-spice, dried apple, double cream, white game and a hint of truffle.

WHERE TO BUY
Via the website or wholesalers and cheesemongers countrywide. See web for details.

WHAT TO DRINK
Rich reds, port, sweet whites and medium cider.

BLUEMIN WHITE

AGE AT RELEASE
6 weeks

STYLE
Soft, Blue

RENNET
Vegetarian

MILK TYPE
Cow

650g

Small Drum

TASTING NOTE
The core holds flavours of rice pudding and chestnut, intensifying to mushroom broth at the rind.

WHERE TO BUY
Via the website or wholesalers and cheesemongers countrywide. See web for details.

WHAT TO DRINK
Medium to rich reds, tawny port, sweet whites, medium cider.

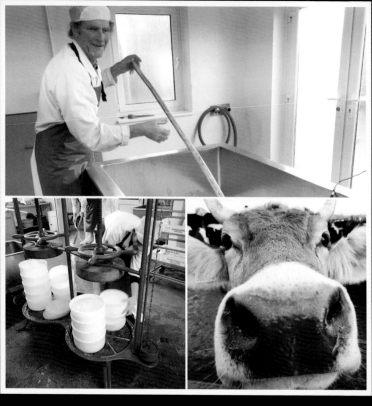

Rod Smart

SMART'S

Founded by Diana Smart in 1985, Smart's Cheese was to be a retirement project, something to add diversity and interest to the dairy farm she had lived on since the age of five, allowing her to step aside from the business of milking and leave it to the next generation.

That next generation, Rod Smart, cheesemaker, and wife Jo are now at the helm of a thriving family business that would not exist but for Diana's forward-thinking decision. One reason for their continued success is the effort the family puts into creating their Gloucester cheeses, to a recipe Diana had been given by a retiring cheesemaker (at a time when the style was in danger of extinction) as well as selling much of it directly to their customers.

Their Single Gloucester is made in the traditional manner, using skimmed milk from the previous evening mixed with the whole morning's yield. The Double is made only from whole milk and coloured with annatto to denote the difference. Single was once considered the lesser cheese, as skimmed milk imparts a lighter flavour and chalkier texture, making it less suitable for transport. Now Single Gloucester, with its own PDO (Protected Designation of Origin), is made to similar if not higher standards than the better-known Double, the name for which has been appropriated by mass producers. The process of draining curd for Single and Double Gloucester is not dissimilar to Cheddaring, in that the curds are cut into blocks and stacked to assist whey loss. At Smarts they are then hand milled and pressed in Victorian upright presses, a laborious process nowadays rarely practised.

For many years Smart's has been the donor of cheeses for the Cheese Rolling event at Cooper's Hill at Brockworth, where in different heats competitors chase a four kilo Double Gloucester 220 metres to the foot of a very steep hill. The donation nearly had to be withdrawn after the local council threatened to make Diana responsible for any injuries should the unlicensed event continue. Common sense has prevailed, and the 150-year-old tradition continues.

Milk type breed: Gloucester, Meuse-Rhine-Issel, Montbéliarde, Normandie, Simmental

SINGLE GLOUCESTER

 AGE AT RELEASE

1 month

STYLE

Hard

RENNET

Vegetarian

MILK TYPE

Cow: See text

 3.3kg, 1.5kg

 Drum

TASTING NOTE

Lovely mottled surface with a pleasing crumble that emits fresh cream, peanut and lemon zest aromas. A palate marginally darker: seed mix, dried field mushroom and dry stone wall.

WHERE TO BUY

Farm shop, local retail, some national wholesale. See website.

WHAT TO DRINK

Aromatic off-dry whites, light chilled reds, cider and hoppy ales.

DOUBLE GLOUCESTER

 AGE AT RELEASE

6 months

STYLE

Hard

RENNET

Vegetarian

MILK TYPE

Cow: See text

 3.3kg, 1.5kg

 Drum

TASTING NOTE

A semi-brittle cheese with baked cream and hazelnuts on the nose and a crunchy palate of dried fruits and mineral with a light toffee hint.

WHERE TO BUY

Farm shop, local retail, some national wholesale. See website.

WHAT TO DRINK

Mid-bodied reds, semi-sweet whites, malty beer or off-dry cider.

HAREFIELD

 AGE AT RELEASE

18 months

STYLE

Hard

RENNET

Vegetarian

MILK TYPE

Cow: See text

 3.3kg, 1.5kg

 Drum

TASTING NOTE

A wizened member of the family with a quartz character to the core, whose loft-dried apple and toasted nut flavours richen closer to the rind with potent venison biltong, roast cashew and a lasting chilli kick.

WHERE TO BUY

Farm shop, local retail, some national wholesale. See website.

WHAT TO DRINK

Rich reds, tawny port, oloroso sherry, winter ale.

Anita Robinson

SOMERSET CHEESE COMPANY

 @somersetcheeseco

 @somersetcheesec

 www.somersetcheese.co.uk

SOMERSET
CHEESE COMPANY

Farmhouse when applied to cheesemaking is as broad (and loose) as the term Cheddar. A word without regulation, it can cover anything from the output of a single herd to dairies processing the milk of a hundred farms or more. When applied to a style it blithely refers to the types of cheese that became popular following the dissolution of the monasteries, with the subsequent move to cow's milk cheese and production on farms: these were semi-hard to hard, pressed cheeses that could be over-wintered. These are among Britain's heritage cheeses, styles such as Cheddar, Cheshire and Lancashire, that have sadly become polarised to a handful of speedily-produced, bland staples.

When, in 2005, Philip Rainbow and Anita Robinson began production at the Somerset Cheese Company, it was their aim to reclaim some of the ground lost to commercialism with farmhouse styles. Encouraged to start the partnership by Nicholas Robinson, Anita's husband, the pair had previously made cheese together at a local dairy, just one of a number that Philip had worked at in his forty-year career.

They chanced upon a dairy owned by retiring cheesemaker John Longman, and arranged to rent the space and equipment, including a 2200 litre farmhouse vat, all suited perfectly to the pair's aims. Philip's breadth of knowledge allowed a clarity of purpose that began to conjure the distinct range of farmhouse cheeses they make today. They began with Fosse Way Fleece, a hard sheep's milk cheese named after the nearby Roman road that once linked Lincoln to Exeter. Goat, cow and buffalo milk farmhouse cheeses have followed, all locally named and each milk sourced from a single local farm to preserve consistency of characters and minimise transport and handling.

The Somerset Cheese Company makes twelve tonnes of cheese a year, split across thirteen distinct styles, only one of them a traditional Cheddar. They are matured for a minimum of four months, in line with traditional farmhouse practice, though the cheeses will improve with further cellaring, one of the clear distinctions between commercial faux-farmhouse and the real thing.

PENNARD VALE

AGE AT RELEASE

4 months

STYLE

Semi Hard

RENNET

Vegetarian

MILK TYPE

Goat

2kg, 3.5kg

Drum

TASTING NOTE

Clean goat milk aromas from a chalky core and stong dark fungus notes to the rind.

WHERE TO BUY

Via the website and retailers and wholesalers in the Southwest. See web for details.

WHAT TO DRINK

Light to medium reds, aromatic whites, hoppy ales, dry cider.

FOSSE WAY

 AGE AT RELEASE
4 months

STYLE
Hard

RENNET
Vegetarian

MILK TYPE
Sheep

2kg, 3.5kg

Drum

TASTING NOTE
An enticing nose of warm cream and seared white meat leads to a fine-grain palate with barley-broth, undergrowth and wild mushroom. Outstanding.

WHERE TO BUY
Via the website and retailers and wholesalers in the Southwest. See web for details.

WHAT TO DRINK
Off-dry sparkling, aromatic white, mid-bodied fruity red, session ale, dry cider.

PENDRAGON BUFFALO

 AGE AT RELEASE

4 months

STYLE

Hard

RENNET

Vegetarian

MILK TYPE

Buffalo

2kg, 3.5kg

Drum

TASTING NOTE

A strong, musky palate of soured cream, spice and fermented cabbage at the core, spicier and dry-mushroom like at the rind.

WHERE TO BUY

Via the website and retailers and wholesalers in the Southwest. See web for details.

WHAT TO DRINK

Medium-bodied reds, rich whites, strong ales and cider.

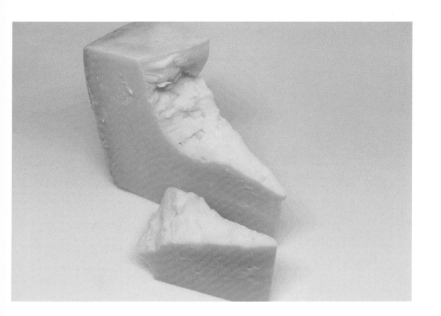

RAINBOWS GOLD

AGE AT RELEASE
6 months

STYLE
Hard, Washed Rind

RENNET
Vegetarian

MILK TYPE
Cow

 2kg, 3.5kg

 Drum

TASTING NOTE

The soft-paste core gives sweet cashew and warm cream flavours, changing at the rind to high mushroom and hung game.

WHERE TO BUY

Via the website and retailers and wholesalers in the Southwest. See web for details.

WHAT TO DRINK

Off-dry whites, medium-bodied reds, malty ale, off-dry cider.

Jane Stewart

ST ANDREWS

:camera: @standrewsfarmhousecheese

:card_file_box: www.standrewscheese.co.uk

ST ANDREWS

ANSTRUTHER, FIFE

As well as good milk, the one thing all Britain's artisan cheesemakers require to make great cheese is passion. Without this vital driver to propel a cheesemaking business beyond the preliminary and uncertain profit-and-loss forecast, very few of our finest cheesemaking businesses would exist. It's not a get-rich-quick industry, if at all.

Along with passion, necessity is also a factor pushing some towards cheesemaking, and so it was with Jane Stewart. In the early 2000s milk production on the Stewarts' mixed arable and dairy farm at Falside was becoming unsustainable due to low milk prices. Her husband's family had been farming the pastures overlooking the Firth of Forth since the 1930s, and Jane once herself worked on a dairy round, so diversification was imperative rather than give up the herd and waste the grassy resource proffered by the rich soils, often mist-laden but balmier than in other parts.

Jane had heard of a retiring cheesemaker in Wales who had equipment for sale so sought him out. From Leon Downey, producer of Llangloffan cheese, she acquired more than the 1000 litre vat, iron presses, peg mill and traditional moulds; she was given a crash course in the production of the recipe with which to start her own enterprise.

Beyond the recipe, she wanted to best express the character of their farm, for which she felt unpasteurised milk was essential, and to make cheese that was faithful to traditional methods. So she employed 'heritage' starter cultures (ancient strains classically used for farmhouse cheese) and animal rennet. In January 2008 Anster emerged, a moist and crumbly Cheshire style recipe, aged for 2-4 months. Cheddar followed, a similar recipe but a warmer make and harder-pressed. Apart from creating smoked and annatto-coloured versions of the two cheeses, that's where Jane stopped, wishing to specialise in 'territorials' (crumbly and pressed cheeses, the styles native to the British Isles).

Aware that to gain the best value from their new cheeses they would have to connect with their public, they installed a farm shop and café, and these together with local farmers' markets comprise the basis of most of their sales. Two of her three sons, Ben and Adam, are now part of the business, family often being the cornerstone for any farm wishing to diversify long term. It's hard to recruit passion externally, especially when farming and cheesemaking are dawn-to-dusk operations.

ANSTER

AGE AT RELEASE	TASTING NOTE
2-4 months	A well made cheese with a clean chalky texture giving apple acid freshness and flavours of lighly spiced cinnamon cream, richening towards the rind with stone-mineral and fungus notes.
STYLE	
Hard	
RENNET	
Animal	WHERE TO BUY
MILK TYPE	Farmers' markets and wholesalers and cheesemongers countrywide. See web for details.
Cow: Holstein Friesian	
14kg	WHAT TO DRINK
Large Drum	Aromatic off-dry whites, light chilled reds, cider and hoppy ales.

FARMOUSE VINTAGE

AGE AT RELEASE

9 months

STYLE

Hard

RENNET

Animal

MILK TYPE

Cow: Holstein
Friesian

14kg

Large Drum

TASTING NOTE

A bold cheese with a crystal-crumble yielding dark notes of game, hot butter and Brazil nut with a pepper bite.

WHERE TO BUY

Farmers' markets and wholesalers and cheesemongers countrywide. See web for details.

WHAT TO DRINK

Sweet whites, rich reds, vintage port, malty ale, cider, whisky.

Martin Gott

ST JAMES CHEESE

 @martingott

www.stjamescheese.co.uk

ST JAMES CHEESE

The path to becoming one of Britain's most iconic cheesemakers began at London's Borough Market for Cumbrian Martin Gott.

While helping on his family farm's meat stall in his teens, he encountered the world's cheese styles as well as some of their makers. A meeting with James Aldridge (a prominent figure in the 1980s movement towards reviving farmhouse cheeses) set Martin's father upon cheesemaking trials at the farm and, though nothing came of the trials, getting his hands into curd as a willing helper lured Martin from beef to dairy. He took up an apprenticeship at Kirkham's Lancashire and while there he met the late Mary Holbrook, a Somerset goat's milk cheesemaker who informed him she wished to stop production. Sensing a chance to maintain a classic as well as get hands-on experience of animal husbandry, he and partner Nicola offered to help. It was there they began making St James (in homage to James Aldridge, who died in 2001) from a small flock of sheep he and Nicola reared. After a year with Mary, in 2006 they moved to their current site on the Holker Estate in Cumbria. (Mary Holbrook continued making cheese at Sleight Farm with assistance from others right up until her death in 2019.)

Now, from a herd of 200 Lacaune sheep (the breed responsible for Roquefort amongst others), Martin and Nicola still make St James, one of the country's most exciting cheeses. They learned from their mentors that distinctive flavour comes from the environment in which the cheese is made. The soil, grass, breed and atmosphere give a unique combination incomparable when minimal intervention is practised. In their pursuit of a taste of place, for St James the marshy pastures of Cartmel, they make their cheese using the farm's own starter cultures rather than buying them in, an elaborate and time-consuming process that enhances the cheese's authenticity.

After a quick-set and moulding like the Alpine cheese Reblochon, the curd then acidifies slowly before salting, encouraging the development of its soft core. The cheeses then undergo regular brine washing for the first fortnight to promote the bacteria that express themselves in the pinky orange colour and pungent flavour.

Martin's pursuit of excellence leads him around the world seeking innovations to bring back not only to Holker Farm but, in keeping with those who inspired him, to the industry as a whole.

ST JAMES

 AGE AT RELEASE

6 weeks

STYLE

Semi Soft, Washed
Rind

RENNET

Animal

MILK TYPE

Sheep: Lacaune

 1.8kg

 Square

TASTING NOTE

The lactic core gives a pleasing break that emits high-
tone floral notes with hints of peanut and fresh grass.
The core palate has a myriad of field flavours, herb,
seed and fresh grass, that interveave with chanterelle,
sweetened game and spice from the rind. Outstanding.

WHERE TO BUY

Wholesalers and cheesemongers countrywide.

WHAT TO DRINK

Semi-sweet white, mead, malty ale.

Joe Schneider

STICHELTON

@sticheltondairy

@sticheltondairy

www.stichelton.co.uk

STICHELTON

⊙ CUCKNEY, NOTTINGHAMSHIRE

Stichelton is the result of a fusion of two strong mindsets firmly aligned to confront another.

Had Randolph Hodgson been contented when in 1988 the last raw milk Stilton producer turned to pasteurised milk for production, Stichelton cheese would not exist. In 2004 he approached American Joe Schneider (who had helped the Bamfords at Daylesford Farm develop their range) with a proposition: Randolph wanted to make a raw milk Stilton, something that also appealed to Joe's belief that the taste of place was lost in the process of pasteurisation.

The Stilton Cheesemakers Association had included pasteurisation as an obligatory process in the Stilton cheese certification and PDO (Protected Designation of Origin), after the detrimental commercial impact on the name Stilton around a health scare in the late 1980s. On being asked by Randolph and Joe whether they might be allowed to join and produce an unpasteurised version, the Association answered no. Some argue that Stilton has become a brand, owned, developed and protected by the Association since its inception in 1936, and without which its name would not have the reputation for quality it enjoys today. Others believe it is a territorial style that should sit beyond above commercial considerations. So Randolph and Joe christened their cheese Stichelton (Stichl: style & Tun: hamlet), an old name for Stilton taken from a twelfth-century record of village names.

Joe and his team are based at Collingthwaite Farm on the Welbeck Estate at the northern edge of Sherwood Forest, Nottinghamshire, one of the three counties, along with Leicestershire and Derbyshire, permitted to make Stilton. They take only the morning milk, warm from the cow, to create a 24 hour-make incarnation of the style. Slowly acidified and painstakingly hand-ladled, the curd is hand-milled one cheese at a time on the second day.

On the shelves, there is a policy of spiking the cheeses late, only allowing air passage to the Penicillium roqueforti within once the curd has developed its creamy flavours, enhancing the complexity of Stichelton. Each cheese is selected for release by taste rather than strict date rotation, as the raw milk has a distinct effect upon each batch; its maturity, texture and flavour differ depending on conditions affecting the microflora in the feed on the day prior to milking. The team creates only 36 cheeses a day, a sliver by comparison with the largest Stilton producers, but it's all quickly spoken for.

STICHELTON

AGE AT RELEASE

4 months

STYLE

Semi Hard, Blue

RENNET

Animal

MILK TYPE

Cow: Holstein
Friesian

8kg

Cylinder

TASTING NOTE

A beast of a blue with high-tone Christmas spice, caramel and butter-fried seeds on the core and a powerful rind that should be approached with a knife and fork: game stock, venison, trompette de la mort mushrooms and the persistent scent of salami. Outstanding.

WHERE TO BUY

Wholesalers and cheesemongers countrywide. See web for details.

WHAT TO DRINK

Rich reds, port, sweet whites and sweet cider.

Sally and Andrew Hattan

STONEBECK

STONEBECK

———————————

Andrew and Sally Hattan are creating a joined-up narrative for their 460-acre farm on the rolling moorland of Nidderdale.

As first-generation tenant farmers, they were aware that they would need to pursue sustainable practices with their small herd of Northern Dairy Shorthorn cows. With just fifteen of the low-yielding cows, once ubiquitous in the Dales, their herd represents a significant proportion of the remaining worldwide population.

They settled upon artisan cheese production and reviving raw milk single farmhouse Wensleydale became their mission, a practice that had died out in the fifties. With the help of Bronwen Percival of Neal's Yard Dairy and Andy Swinscoe at the Courtyard Dairy, the couple researched pre-war Wensleydale techniques and interviewed cheesemakers from the time who were able to pass on recipes and guidance the pair have absorbed and moulded into the ever-refining template for their Stonebeck cheese.

Not happy simply with authenticity of livestock and recipe, they are working hard on what they see as the key element, the quality of the milk. To this end they are ensuring the feed provides further local narrative to the story told on the palate. Virtually all their year-round feed comes from grass from their own pastures and meadows. These they are re-wilding with flowers and plants once native to the area, knowing full well that this sensitive and sustainable approach will repay them handsomely in the complexity of flavour in their authentic, calico-bound, raw milk, Wensleydale cheese. A worthy mouthful in every sense.

WENSLEYDALE

 AGE AT RELEASE
6 weeks

STYLE
Hard

RENNET
Animal

MILK TYPE
Cow: Shorthorn

 3kg

Drum

TASTING NOTE

The creamy buttercup-yellow core gives pungent flavours of roasted cashew, chanterelle and toffee, whilst the rind, a meal in itself, lends the experience a platter of wild boar charcuterie. Outstanding.

WHERE TO BUY

See web for details.

WHAT TO DRINK

Aromatic off-dry whites, chilled fruity reds, cider and hoppy ales.

Jason and Katharine Salisbury

SUFFOLK FARMHOUSE CHEESES

@suffolkcheese

@suffolkcheese

www.suffolkcheese.co.uk

SUFFOLK FARMHOUSE CHEESES

⊙ CREETING ST MARY, SUFFOLK

In the sixteenth century the county of Suffolk developed a poor reputation for cheese because much of its milk was destined for butter or cream, leaving only skimmed milk to produce a hard offering, Suffolk Bang, that became a source of derision.

A chance encounter in a Cambridge University dairy parlour in the nineties helped spark a renaissance. It was where Jason and Katharine Salisbury met, he tending the herd, she studying to be a vet. In 2004, after a period in their chosen careers, the herd Jason was managing in Coddenham was put up for sale. Taking the metaphorical bull by the horns, the Salisburys bought a herd of 16 Guernsey cows and started making cheese in rented dairy buildings on site. Three years later, following a cheese course at Reeseheath and with recipes honed, the couple bought Whitegate Farm and began to grow the business and their herd.

Animal welfare, not surprisingly, is at the heart of the operation and the pair have expanded with an awareness that good feed, plenty of space, and a healthy relaxed herd all make for good cheese. The cows are milked robotically with a voluntary milking system. Whilst labour saving, the system saves little cost as the machines need maintenance and the herd still requires the eye of an expert herdsman. The couple believe this is better for animal welfare as it allows the cows to be milked whenever they choose, on average 2.5 times per day.

Suffolk Gold is their flagship offering, the colour describing the core of the cheese: butter-yellow due to the high levels of beta-carotene that Channel Islands breeds are less able to metabolise. Jason and Katherine have added Jerseys to their herd, as well as Ayrshire, all producing milk higher in butterfats, a factor that enhances the creaminess of their cheese.

Sustainability is also key to the success of a modern cheesemaking farm. At Whitegate all male calves are reared on the farm for beef, and the whey from cheesemaking is fed to a 50-strong herd of pigs, the meat of both sold locally to a highly appreciative audience, as Channel Islands beef and whey-fed pork are highly prized. It's the taste and quality of their cheeses however, along with those of a handful of other new producers, that will finally lay the ghost of Suffolk Bang to rest.

SUFFOLK BRIE

AGE AT RELEASE
3 weeks

STYLE
Soft, Bloomy

RENNET
Vegetarian

MILK TYPE
Cow: Jersey, Guernsey, Ayrshire

800g

Disk

TASTING NOTE
Fresh button mushroom broth on the nose and a saline cream core with hints of hazelnut.

WHERE TO BUY
Farm shop or wholesalers and cheesemongers countrywide. See web for details.

WHAT TO DRINK
Sparkling, chilled light red, dry white, cider.

SUFFOLK GOLD

 AGE AT RELEASE

9 weeks

STYLE

Semi Hard

RENNET

Vegetarian

MILK TYPE

Cow: Jersey, Guernsey, Ayrshire

 3kg

Drum

TASTING NOTE

One of the prettiest rinds in cheese, mottled chamois leather-like, with a nose of warm straw, crème de cacao and a basket of wild mushrooms. The palate is gently elastic with meaty notes overlaid with clotted cream and Brazil nut flavours. Outstanding.

WHERE TO BUY

Farm shop or wholesalers and cheesemongers countrywide. See web for details.

WHAT TO DRINK

Aromatic off-dry whites, light chilled reds, cider and hoppy ales.

SUFFOLK BLUE

 AGE AT RELEASE

6 weeks

STYLE

Semi Hard, Blue

RENNET

Vegetarian

MILK TYPE

Cow: Jersey, Guernsey, Ayrshire

 700g

Drum

TASTING NOTE

Lovely mottling to the rind. The core gives aromas of Valencia orange, apricot and cream, while the rind leans to sweet fungus. The palate is sweet and sour with a feisty penicillin kick backed by apple pie, forest nut and pigeon breast flavours. Outstanding.

WHERE TO BUY

Farm shop or wholesalers and cheesemongers countrywide. See web for details.

WHAT TO DRINK

Rich reds, tawny port, sweet whites and dessert gin.

Leonie Fairburn

THORNBY MOOR DAIRY

 @thornbymoor

 www.thornbymoordairy.co.uk

THORNBY MOOR DAIRY

◉ THURSBY, CUMBRIA

The wild and timeless Solway Coast, overlooking the Irish Sea, teeming with wildlife and dotted with remote farmsteads, was never a source of cheese but rather of milk and particularly fine butter, often used in the spiced cakes the area is still noted for. So, in 1979, when Carolyn Fairburn, a photographer by profession, chose to make a little cheese from the surplus milk of their smallholding's goats, there were few rules to follow.

Setting herself up in the basement of the family's Solway bank farmhouse, the room historically used to house cattle, she set about creating her own recipe for a semi-hard cheese that she named Allerdale, after the local district. At first it was simply a calling fuelled by a desire to provide something nutritious for the family and sell to those she knew with cow's milk intolerances. Allerdale proved popular however and the herd increased in size to accommodate demand.

In her youth in Lavenham, Suffolk, Carolyn had been a dairy promotion girl, selling milk door-to-door from a horse-drawn cart. The herd had been shorthorn and the fondness stayed with her, so when she sought a new style for Thornby Moor she looked to the milk of a local shorthorn herd. Cumberland Farmhouse, the result, is a hard-pressed, cloth-bound cheese that gives great expression to this breed's rich milk.

Other cheeses have followed, including fresh cheeses and smoked versions as well as Crofton, a mixed goat's and cow's milk cheese initially created out of convenience to use up spare milk but now a firm favourite of the area's chefs. Carolyn, joined by daughter Leonie, pursued a policy of selling exclusively to hotels and restaurants, through which she felt they could have more of a connection with the end customer, stressing that cheese is the only single-ingredient course on a menu and it is the memory of the taste that the customer goes home with.

The dairy moved a short way to its current premises in 1994 and the herd sadly went with the foot-and-mouth crisis in 2001. Yet Thornby Moor have preserved their integrity and still source all their milk, unpasteurised, from local single herds. They continue to make their cheeses to the original recipes, allowing these remote pastures to express themselves through produce in a way they hadn't ever done before.

CROFTON

 AGE AT RELEASE
4 weeks

STYLE
Semi Soft

RENNET
Animal

MILK TYPE
Cow & Goat

 800g

 Small Drum

TASTING NOTE
Single cream, hints of hay and citrus on the core richen to milled pepper and dried mushroom on the rind.

WHERE TO BUY
Via the website or wholesalers and cheesemongers countrywide. See web for details.

WHAT TO DRINK
Aromatic off-dry whites, chilled fruity reds, cider and hoppy ales.

TOVEY

AGE AT RELEASE

4 weeks

STYLE

Semi Soft

RENNET

Animal

MILK TYPE

Goat

250g

Small Drum

TASTING NOTE

Chalky and citric with notes of farmyard and goat.

WHERE TO BUY

Via the website or wholesalers and cheesemongers
countrywide. See web for details.

WHAT TO DRINK

Sparkling, chilled light reds, dry white, cider.

BLUE WINNOW

AGE AT RELEASE

8 weeks

STYLE

Semi Hard, Blue

RENNET

Animal

MILK TYPE

Cow: Shorthorn

1kg, 450g

Small Drum

TASTING NOTE

A piquant bundle of blue spice with aromas of grilled walnut
and rich cream, and pleasing earthy pepper and dried fruit on
the palate.

WHERE TO BUY

Via the website or wholesalers and cheesemongers
countrywide. See web for details.

WHAT TO DRINK

Medium to rich reds, tawny port, sweet whites, medium cider.

ALLERDALE

AGE AT RELEASE

4 months

STYLE

Semi Hard

RENNET

Animal

MILK TYPE

Goat

2kg

Small Drum

TASTING NOTE

Fresh and winey on the nose with hints of undergrowth and a friable palate with game and lemon notes.

WHERE TO BUY

Via the website or wholesalers and cheesemongers countrywide. See web for details.

WHAT TO DRINK

Off-dry sparkling, aromatic white, mid-bodied fruity red.

CUMBERLAND

 AGE AT RELEASE
5 months

STYLE
Hard

RENNET
Animal

MILK TYPE
Cow: Shorthorn

 900g

Small Drum

TASTING NOTE
Sweet vanilla and candy-floss on the nose complementing a semi-elastic palate with notes of macadamia and hay.

WHERE TO BUY
Via the website or wholesalers and cheesemongers countrywide. See web for details.

WHAT TO DRINK
Rich reds, tawny port, sweet whites and dessert gin.

Ben Harris

TICKLEMORE

@ticklemore_cheese_dairy

@benticklemore

www.ticklemorecheese.co.uk

TICKLEMORE

The Ticklemore story started in the seventies when Robin Congdon, a smallholder fascinated by fermentation, started making yoghurt and fresh cheese from the milk of his thirty sheep on his property near Exeter, selling it directly to discerning outlets in London.

An encounter with Maurice Ash of the Sharpham Estate in Totnes spawned a partnership and Robin moved production to the estate, giving him the platform to experiment. He started with blue-veined cheeses which then, apart from Stilton, were a British style largely lost due to the pressures of wartime rationing. Keen to further the niche, he stuck with sheep's milk. A Roquefort style was the natural choice and there he travelled for inspiration. Beenleigh Blue, rindless and foil-wrapped, though a less piquant incarnation of Roquefort, soon found support from Randolph Hodgson of Neal's Yard Dairy, amongst others.

The seasonal nature of Beenleigh Blue (the sheep are dry over winter) led to the development of the goat's milk Harbourne Blue and later cow's milk Devon Blue, both made from purchased milk to a recipe similar to Beenleigh Blue. As the business grew the flock was sold, the focus shifting from farming to cheesemaking, and the dairy separated from Sharpham. Robin moved production to a ridge a little way to the west, overlooking the Dart Valley and the Sharpham Estate. Other cheeses emerged, including the goat's milk Ticklemore, the recipe for which passed to the Sharpham Estate with the decision to consolidate the range on Robin's semi-retirement in 2008.

Ben Harris, a dairy farmer's son and former chef is now head cheesemaker, a dynamic character who, whilst aware of the legacy he has taken on, continues to innovate, having to respond daily to the changing composition of three milks as well as the seasonal demands of a marketplace eager for more cheese than the dairy is able to produce.

BEENLEIGH BLUE

AGE AT RELEASE

3 months

STYLE

Semi Hard, Blue

RENNET

Vegetarian

MILK TYPE

Sheep

 3.5kg

 Drum

TASTING NOTE

A sweet-cream nose with aromas of dried pear and nutmeg and a crumbly palate with a piquant pepper and cox apple bite.

WHERE TO BUY

See website for details.

WHAT TO DRINK

Medium reds, tawny port, sweet whites and medium cider.

HARBOURNE BLUE

 AGE AT RELEASE

3 months

STYLE

Semi Hard, Blue

RENNET

Vegetarian

MILK TYPE

Goat

3.5kg

Drum

TASTING NOTE

The chalky crumble releases fresh citric notes followed by a gentle goat-musk and cumin aromas. A pleasing initial bite to the palate recedes to give a creamy paste threaded with pepper spice and walnut. Outstanding.

WHERE TO BUY

See website for details.

WHAT TO DRINK

Off-dry sparkling, sweet whites, mid-bodied fruity red.

DEVON BLUE

AGE AT RELEASE

3 months

STYLE

Semi Hard, Blue

RENNET

Vegetarian

MILK TYPE

Cow: Friesian

3.5kg

Drum

TASTING NOTE

The cheese seduces you with high-tone pistachio cream and curry spice aromas, and on the palate the even crumble easily yields to give a rich saline-cream-crunch with flavours of rice pudding, baked plum, apricot and Victoria sponge. Exceptional.

WHERE TO BUY

See website for details.

WHAT TO DRINK

Rich reds, port, sweet whites and medium cider.

Cliff Dyball

TRADITIONAL CHEESE DAIRY

@thetraditionalcheesedairy

www.thetraditionalcheesedairy.com

TRADITIONAL CHEESE DAIRY

◎ STONEGATE, EAST SUSSEX

The business model for the Traditional Cheese Dairy is a template for aspiring cheesemakers who wish to concentrate on crafting fine cheese rather than take on the considerable responsibilities of animal husbandry.

In better established cheesemaking countries much artisan cheese is made by purchasing milk from farmers, allowing each constituent to specialise in just one of these two very different disciplines. Cliff and Julie Dyball and their daughter Becky bought the business in 2001 from a regional distributor and began to expand the range and improve the milk sources, understanding it to be the key to developing quality.

The cheeses are crafted out of raw milk from single farms that prioritise milk quality over volume. This has helped the Dyballs produce more flavoursome cheeses that can command a premium, which feeds back to the farm, supporting its longevity, and in turn nurtures the local economy, animal welfare and the palates of those who can track the cheeses down.

Burwash Rose has become a local classic. Washed in a solution of brine and rosewater, the rind of the cheese takes on the pungent sweet-feet aromas associated with the washed-rind style, tempered with a gentle perfume.

LORD OF THE HUNDREDS

 AGE AT RELEASE

8 months

STYLE

Hard

RENNET

Vegetarian

MILK TYPE

Cow: Viking Red,
Holstein Friesian

 3.6kg

 Square

TASTING NOTE

Elegant farmyard and cashew nuts on the nose with a
crumbly palate giving dried stone fruit, hay and lanolin
notes.

WHERE TO BUY

Wholesalers and cheesemongers countrywide. See
website.

WHAT TO DRINK

Aromatic off-dry whites, light reds, cider and hoppy
ales.

BURWASH ROSE

 AGE AT RELEASE

6 weeks

STYLE

Soft, Washed Rind

RENNET

Vegetarian

MILK TYPE

Cow: Viking Red,
Holstein Friesian

800g

Disk

TASTING NOTE

Ripe gamey nose with peanut butter and floral notes and a
creamy core of mushroom broth and clotted cream.

WHERE TO BUY

Wholesalers and cheesemongers countrywide. See website.

WHAT TO DRINK

Semi-sweet white, medium-bodied reds, off-dry cider, malty
ale.

BROADOAK
CHEDDAR

 AGE AT RELEASE

12 months

STYLE

Hard

RENNET

Vegetarian

MILK TYPE

Cow: Viking Red,
Holstein Friesian

14kg

Large Drum

TASTING NOTE

A tangy mouthful of woodland flavours.

WHERE TO BUY

Wholesalers and cheesemongers countrywide. See website.

WHAT TO DRINK

Sweet whites, rich reds, tawny port, malty ale, strong cider.

Maugan Trethowan

@ @trethowansdairy

🐦 @trethowansdairy

🗂 www.trethowanbrothers.com

TRETHOWAN'S DAIRY

Though Caerphilly is one of our British territorial cheeses, little now is faithful to the farm tradition that brought the name to fame.

A young, crumbly, brine-bathed cheese, it became popular with the miners of South Wales in the early 19th century, who were keen to replace lost salt in their diet. It was made on farm, in small batches and from raw milk. The style spread from Wales to the West Country and adopted the name of the Welsh market town where it was regularly traded.

The story of Trethowans Dairy also straddles the Severn Estuary. In 1996, fresh from Somerset and a spell working with Chris Duckett at Duckett's Caerphilly (one of the few producers to return to traditional methods after the style was prohibited during rationing), Todd Trethowan began making Gorwydd Caerphilly with bought-in milk on his parents' sheep farm at Llanddewi Brefi on the edge of the Cambrian Mountains. Todd was keen to create a complex style and began making four cheeses a day from unpasteurised milk, eventually allowing it to develop a mould rind to add complexity.

The business grew to envelop wife Jess, brother Maugan and sister-in-law Kim, and by the time they had been making it for eighteen years it had rightly become a benchmark for the style. But in 2014 inconsistency of milk supply coupled with a desire for expansion necessitated change. They moved production to Puxton Farm in Somerset, not far from where Todd had learned his craft at Duckett's and, ironically, significantly closer to the town of Caerphilly than the family's remote Welsh hill farm.

The benefit of this relocation was a source of supply they could control, from an entrepreneurial farmer who would gain from the partnership by means of a guaranteed fair price for the output of his high-welfare herd, something the bulk milk market was increasingly failing to offer. Keen to maintain the signature flavours in Gorwydd, every effort was made to ensure there'd be no loss of quality with the move, including inoculating the maturation walls with moulds from the original cellar. The dairy now sits opposite the cow parlour, the milk gravity-fed into the vats, ensuring minimal manipulation of the milk prior to production.

With their new dairy just seven miles from the town that spawned the world's biggest name in cheese, the choice to create a Cheddar was a natural one for the Trethowans. True to the mindset that has helped restore pride to the Caerphilly name, Pitchfork Cheddar is a traditional, unpasteurised, cloth-bound incarnation, joining only a handful still upholding the farmhouse tradition of another great British territorial.

GORWYDD CAERPHILLY

 AGE AT RELEASE

10 weeks

STYLE

Semi Hard

RENNET

Animal

MILK TYPE

Cow: Holstein Friesian, Jersey

 2kg, 4kg

 Drum

TASTING NOTE

On the nose, the white dusted rind gives mushroom broth and stone notes whilst the under-rind is yeasty cream and hazelnut, turning grassier and citric at the crumbly core, with flavours that follow suit. Exceptional.

WHERE TO BUY

Wholesalers and cheesemongers countrywide. See web for details.

WHAT TO DRINK

Sparkling, aromatic whites, light reds, hoppy ale and cider.

PITCHFORK CHEDDAR

AGE AT RELEASE

12 months

STYLE

Hard

RENNET

Animal

MILK TYPE

Cow: Holstein
Friesian, Jersey

25kg

Large Drum

TASTING NOTE

A moreish and complex cheddar with a creamy core of toasted nuts, wholegrain and marmite hints with mineral and dry forest floor flavours at the rind. Exceptional.

WHERE TO BUY

Wholesalers and cheesemongers countrywide. See web for details.

WHAT TO DRINK

Sweet whites, rich reds, vintage port, malty ale, cider, whisky.

Alistair Rodgers

TREVEADOR
FARM DAIRY

@treveadorfarmdairy

www.treveadorfarmdairy.com

TREVEADOR FARM DAIRY

The inspiration for the unique range at Treveador Farm Dairy began with a desire to create something more than just milk, a commodity that left the farm gates and was then quickly forgotten.

Alastair Rodgers had been dairy farming on the salt-sprayed slopes of Condurrow Farm, overlooking the mouth of the Helford River, since the age of 16 and, approaching 50, he decided it was time for a change. He had toyed with ice cream making in the 1990s but found it unsatisfactory as he found it difficult to create something distinctive, so in 2001 he accepted a farm diversification grant and spent it on a cheesemaking course with Chris Ashby in Leicestershire.

The course furthered interest, but it wasn't until 2006, after his son Jon took over running the herd, that he and partner Bernadette Newman began to experiment with some recipes given to them by Chris. The first cheeses were, by Alastair's admission, less than saleable (not unusual in cheese development) but with the assistance of French consultant, Ivan Larcher, within a year they were ready to go to market.

They chose to specialise in soft cheeses, the first of which were Helford Blue and Helford White, the latter loosely modelled on reblochon, its washed rind giving it a gentle pink colour. Since moving to their current premises in Helston in 2012, the range has expanded to include Helford Camembert and Helford Sunrise. Sunrise is a richer version of Helford White, its rind coloured with annatto (an orange pigment derived from the seeds of the achiote tree, native to South America) and washed in Helford Creek cider every three days during maturation before being sprinkled with crushed peppercorns. As with most drink adjuncts, the cider is not added to flavour the rind but to provide nutrients for the rind-bound bacteria, assisting its development and the breakdown of the curd beneath. The alcohol, generally diluted to below 4% ABV, also acts as a suppressant of unwanted moulds.

Alastair considers cheesemaking akin to retirement compared with dairy farming, and a pursuit he wished he had taken up sooner. Jon now farms 300 cows, 90% of the milk from which is still destined for the wholesale market. However father and son take great pleasure from the remaining 10% that provides a connection with their public and the rewarding smiles derived directly from their endeavours.

HELFORD WHITE

AGE AT RELEASE

3 weeks

STYLE

Soft, Washed Rind

RENNET

Vegetarian

MILK TYPE

Cow: H.F.
Montbéliarde

1kg, 200g, 100g

Disk, Small Disk

TASTING NOTE

On the nose the core gives a clean and fragrant lemon cream aroma with hints of parsley. The rind is a completely different proposition, with rich peanut butter on toast and gentle toffee aromas. On the palate, the core is crumbly and lemon-lactic and again the rind impresses with a brash display of white game stock, light spice and salted bacon. Outstanding.

WHERE TO BUY

Wholesalers and cheesemongers locally. See web for details.

WHAT TO DRINK

Off-dry whites, light reds, hoppy ale, off-dry cider.

HELFORD SUNRISE

 AGE AT RELEASE

3 weeks

STYLE

Soft, Washed Rind

RENNET

Vegetarian

MILK TYPE

Cow: H.F.
Montbéliarde

 1kg, 250g

 Disk, Small Disk

TASTING NOTE

A slippery, pleasantly rubbery paste giving diverse aromas of
sweet cream, toffee, christmas spice and honey cashew. Earthier
on the rind with salami and peppercorn notes. Outstanding.

WHERE TO BUY

Wholesalers and cheesemongers locally. See web for details.

WHAT TO DRINK

Off-dry whites, full-bodied reds, malty ale, ciders.

HELFORD BLUE

AGE AT RELEASE

3 weeks

STYLE

Soft, Blue

RENNET

Vegetarian

MILK TYPE

Cow: H.F.
Montbéliarde

 1kg, 250g, 150g

Disk, Small Disk

TASTING NOTE

Semi-soft and savoury core giving balanced pepper-spice with
white meats, horse mushroom and dusty cream; richer mineral
and dried hazelnut notes on the rind.

WHERE TO BUY

Wholesalers and cheesemongers locally. See web for details.

WHAT TO DRINK

Medium reds, tawny port, sweet whites and medium cider.

Sandy Rose

TWO HOOTS CHEESE

TWO HOOTS CHEESE

Two Hoots, named after a pair of owls rescued on a former smallholding owned by Sandy and Andy Rose, is a model for anyone wishing to understand what defines success in the artisan cheese world as well as what makes a great artisan cheese.

The foundation for Two Hoots began in Sandy's youth. Growing up on a dairy farm in Shurlock Row she developed a love of Guernsey cows and an appreciation of the high quality of their milk. Her path to cheese, however, was to be via goats and the smallholding she bought with husband Andy in the eighties. Encouraged by her cousin Anne Wigmore of nearby Village Maid, Sandy began to make cheese in a bucket and drained the curds above the bath. The resulting fresh goat's cheese was blended with garlic and chives, a prototype that went on to be sold at farmers' markets.

An award-winning brie style followed but Sandy craved a cheese unique to Two Hoots. Her passion for Geurnseys and a love of blue cheese combined to set her experimenting. She was told that for a blue cheese Guernsey milk would be hard to work with as the high fat content would make draining difficult and thus create poor conditions for the development of mold. It takes skill to make a blue, let alone one from butterfat-rich milk, but rather than be put off, Sandy saw this as a reason to pursue her course. It didn't take long for her to crack the secret as six months later Barkham Blue won Best New Cheese at the 2003 World Cheese Awards.

Nearly two decades on the cheese remains unique. No other cheese looks or tastes quite like it. The temptation to scale up or sell out after the multiple awards Barkham Blue has won must have been great, but the pair has stuck to a family business model that works for them, and for the cheeses, realising the dedication that goes into creating the 500 rounds a week might not be easily scalable. Those who love this cheese must be content with getting hold of a little whenever they can.

BARKHAM BLUE

 AGE AT RELEASE

5 weeks

STYLE

Semi Hard, Blue

RENNET

Vegetarian

MILK TYPE

Cow: Guernsey

 850g

 Ammonite

TASTING NOTE

A moreish buttery texture holds well balanced flavours of crème caramel, macadamia nut and warm straw threaded with a complementary blue piquancy. Outstanding.

WHERE TO BUY

Wholesalers and cheesemongers countrywide. See website.

WHAT TO DRINK

Rich off-dry reds, sweet whites, tawny port and dessert gin.

Anne and Andy Wigmore

VILLAGE MAID CHEESE

@villagemaidcheese

@villagemaid

www.villagemaidcheese.co.uk

VILLAGE MAID CHEESE

Three generations now have a hand on the vat at Village Mail Dairy in Riseley, Berkshire, but it was middle generation Anne Wigmore that was responsible for the inception of this innovative and consistently high-achieving producer. Dedication and hard work can only count for so much, and those the family and their team exhibit in abundance, but Anne's background in microbiology helped propel Village Maid's cheeses to the top tier early on. Following studies in dairy science and a decade at the National Institute for Research in Dairying, in 1986 Anne decided to go it alone after a sabbatical during which she assisted husband Andy on an adventure to sail a self-made yacht to Australia.

Inspired by Pecorino Sardo, a hard sheep's cheese she had encountered in Sardinia while on the trip, she began producing Spenwood in a shed at the foot of the garden. Other cheeses soon followed, including a Cheddar-recipe cheese made from milk of the Duke of Wellington's Guernsey herd. Production of 'Wellington' ceased with the Duke's retirement, but working with Channel Island breed milk gave Anne the inspiration for Waterloo, their bloomy-rind cheese also made from Guernsey milk. After a move to their current premises in Riseley, Anne created a soft sheep's cheese to the style of Waterloo for Neal's Yard Dairy, which they named Wigmore, much to Anne's blushes. Wigmore has become one of the most highly awarded British cheeses, including twice Best English Cheese at the British Cheese Awards. Her others aren't far behind.

Anne was a pioneer at a time when there were few artisan cheesemakers in the country, and whilst she and Andy remain drivers of the business, innovation continues to flow from son Jake and partner Kayleigh. They've come up with a cheese in a size and shape like Waterloo and Wigmore but with a hue, smell and taste markedly different. The key to this is a regime of rind-washing in ale from a local brewery. The quality of Maida Vale, a play on words rather than homage to the London district of Paddington, has added a new dimension to the dairy that should see the awards tally continue to grow.

WIGMORE

AGE AT RELEASE
6 weeks

STYLE
Soft, Bloomy

RENNET
Vegetarian

MILK TYPE
Sheep

180g, 350g, 750g

Small Disk, Disk

TASTING NOTE
Clean flavours of button mushroom from the rind give way to straw and fresh seed on the palate.

WHERE TO BUY
Via website or wholesalers and cheesemongers countrywide. See web for details.

WHAT TO DRINK
Sparkling, chilled light red, dry white, cider.

WATERLOO

AGE AT RELEASE
6 weeks

STYLE
Soft, Bloomy

RENNET
Vegetarian

MILK TYPE
Cow: Guernsey

180g, 350g, 750g

Small Disk, Disk

TASTING NOTE
Aromas of mushroom broth on the rind and a warm buttery palate.

WHERE TO BUY
Via website or wholesalers and cheesemongers countrywide. See web for details.

WHAT TO DRINK
Off-dry sparkling or white, light & fruity red.

SPENWOOD

AGE AT RELEASE
6 months

STYLE
Hard

RENNET
Vegetarian

MILK TYPE
Sheep

2kg

Drum

TASTING NOTE
The powerful yet elegant fine-grain core gives lasting notes of dried orchard fruit and pressed flowers. Outstanding.

WHERE TO BUY
Via website or wholesalers and cheesemongers countrywide. See web for details.

WHAT TO DRINK
Off-dry sparkling, aromatic white, mid-bodied fruity red.

MAIDA VALE

AGE AT RELEASE
6 weeks

STYLE
Soft, Washed Rind

RENNET
Vegetarian

MILK TYPE
Cow: Guernsey, Jersey

350g

Small Disk, Disk

TASTING NOTE
Pralines and cream on the nose lead to a palate of dried apricot, winged game and spice.

WHERE TO BUY
Via website or wholesalers and cheesemongers countrywide. See web for details.

WHAT TO DRINK
Light red, semi-sweet white or malty ale.

Margaret Callow and Andrew Ruddle

WEBSTERS

🖿 www.webstersdairy.co.uk

WEBSTERS

Travel is at the core of Websters Dairy ethos, one of the reasons contributing to the scarcity of this little-encountered Stilton.

The gourmet wanderings of owners Margaret and Helen Callow have led to more than 70% of their production going overseas, which is why only the most determined will get to taste their Stilton. The other reason for its rarity is that their dairy, situated in a seventeenth century row of cottages in the hamlet of Saxelby, is the smallest of the six Stilton producers, accounting for only a tiny fraction of the over one million Stiltons produced annually.

Started by the Webster sisters in the mid-nineteenth century, the cheesemaking dairy was bought by Margaret and Helen's father in 1979. The Callow sisters had grown up with cheese, their father having been a wholesaler and devotee of traditional cloth-bound Cheddar after the war, a rare sight back then. Margaret is now at the helm, but her progression into the business was not assured, their entrepreneur father keen to have the girls make their own way. After ten years as a laboratory technician, Margaret returned, her training bringing new skills and her innate attention to detail helping to elevate consistency. This was an important factor as the style is among the most difficult to perfect, the key being to get the curd texture correct for Penicillium roqueforti to develop blue veining evenly throughout the cheese.

The dairy buys milk in from six small dairies, and at a premium that supports their continued viability. In turn their milk allows the flavours of this quiet corner of northern Leicestershire to be discovered and treasured wherever the Callow walking boot may tread.

STILTON

 AGE AT RELEASE

4 months

STYLE

Semi Hard, Blue

RENNET

Vegetarian

MILK TYPE

Cow: Holstein
Friesian

 8kg

Cylinder

TASTING NOTE

A pungent blue with Roquefort-like bite and rich
salted-cream core.

WHERE TO BUY

See web for details.

WHAT TO DRINK

Rich reds, port, sweet whites and medium cider.

Tom Calver

WESTCOMBE DAIRY

:camera: @westcombecheese

:bird: @westcombedairy

:calendar: www.westcombedairy.com

WESTCOMBE DAIRY

Somerset is not cheesemaking country by accident. The county grows one crop as well as any part of the world. The low hills, warm microclimates, generous rainfall, gentle mists and rich soils conspire to provide the one ingredient perfect for plentiful cheese-grade milk: rich grass. When that grass is allowed to grow in a way that benefits cheese diversity, with minimal chemical intervention and an understanding that quality is made in the field and not the dairy, then the conditions for creating cheese magic are set. It's a magic that's happening once again at Westcombe.

Cheesemaking began at Westcombe in 1879 under Edith Cannon. It was then an unremarkable feat, as hundreds of farmers' wives would have generated a winter store for their mixed farm. In the early 1900s the Bicknell family expanded upon this, and by the time second-generation Phyllis Bicknell was in charge, Cheddar was being produced from the milk of three herds in the Westcombe district.

Traditional cheesemaking at the farm had weathered the war years, but by the time Richard Calver joined in the 1960s the farm had moved with the times to block Cheddar. Richard gradually took on the farming and joined Phyllis in partnership, later taking over cheesemaking duties. By the early 1990s competition in the commodity Cheddar market forced a re-think. Westcombe went back to its roots in joining the tiny number of Somerset cheesemakers still producing traditionally Cheddared, unpasteurised, cloth-bound Cheddar. It was a decision that Richard's son, Tom Calver, acknowledges saved the farm. A chef by trade, Tom took over in 2008, with a desire to build upon what his father had started. His experiences with world cheeses and an apprenticeship at Neal's Yard Dairy had shown him the scope of what might be possible for Cheddar. Innovations in the fields, dairy and maturation room followed. Higher methods of animal welfare, a move towards natural fertilisers, gentler handling of the milk, and a new underground maturation cave have all contributed to the quality of the cheeses.

The moulds on long-aged, hard, naturally-rinded cheeses are attractive to cheese mites. The traditional method of dealing with them is a regular brush down, a laborious manual process. Tom looked to the Jurassic cellars of Comté for inspiration, where complementary mechanisation has been embraced, installing a robotic brusher and turner, nicknamed Tina. Westcombe is one of only four companies to be recognised as producers of Artisan Somerset Cheddar by the slow food movement, in that the cheese is made from unpasteurised milk, using traditional pint starters and animal rennet, hand Cheddared (the process of block-cutting curd whilst it drains) and made into 22kg or larger cloth-bound cheeses. The dairy also produces an unpasteurised and naturally-rinded Caerphilly. Duckett's Caerphilly (named in honour of Chris Duckett, who brought the family recipe to Westcombe in the 1990s) is in the premier tier for the style, matured in its own ageing room, complete with a natural spring to assist temperature and humidity regulation.

Westcombe Dairy is an important mirror to the past as well as a glimpse into the future of Cheddar, the two intrinsically similar despite the shape and shine of methods new.

DUCKETT'S CAERPHILLY

 AGE AT RELEASE
6 months

STYLE
Semi Hard

RENNET
Animal

MILK TYPE
Cow: Ayrshire,
Holstein Friesian

4kg

Small Drum

TASTING NOTE
Three cheeses in one, with an even, chalky-core centre giving gentle notes of lime and grass, with the under-rind breakdown adding notes of clotted cream, before the generous rind provides layers of dried field mushroom flavours. Outstanding.

WHERE TO BUY
Via the website or wholesalers and cheesemongers countrywide. See web for details.

WHAT TO DRINK
Aromatic off-dry whites, light chilled reds, cider and hoppy ales.

CHEDDAR

 AGE AT RELEASE
12 months

STYLE
Hard

RENNET
Animal

MILK TYPE
Cow: Ayrshire,
Holstein Friesian

 25kg

 Drum

TASTING NOTE

The nose gives rich and characterful scents of seed,
vanilla and creamed cashew, which continue through
the rich cream-crunch palate with flavours of summer
hay, dried orchard fruit, becoming stone-mineral-like
towards the rind. Exceptional.

WHERE TO BUY

Via the website or wholesalers and cheesemongers
countrywide. See web for details.

WHAT TO DRINK

Sweet whites, rich reds, vintage port, malty ale, cider,
whisky.

Sue Proudfoot

WHALESBOROUGH CHEESE

Whalesborough Farm was nurturing animals since before the mention of its two cows and fifteen sheep in the Domesday book.

In 1962 Wilfred Proudfoot added a new chapter to the farm's history when, in one day, he transported his young family and herd of Ayrshires to the 500-acre property, spanning the gentle vales snaking down to Bude. In 1999, three generations on, Sue Proudfoot, the archetype polymath farmer's wife, who had supported revenues with egg sales, sheep breeding, care work and even milk churn painting, decided to add cheesemaking to her roles. She learned how to make cheese in her kitchen, using a bain marie as a vat and tractor weights as presses.

Her first creation, Trelawny, a classic farmhouse Cheddar, was an immediate hit locally. Keltic Gold, a younger cheese, rind-washed in local cider, soon joined it on counters and cheeseboards across Cornwall. However, volumes weren't enough to account for a large enough proportion of the output from the farm's then 300 cows, and in 2004 below-cost milk prices, having followed Mad Cow Disease and Foot and Mouth Disease in the late nineties, amassed to a trifecta that proved too overwhelming. The herd had to be sold.

Such was the popularity of Sue's cheeses, and the recognition and awards they were gathering, that the decision to buy milk from a local herd was taken. The range continued to grow and so too volumes, and in 2009 the dairy moved to Norton Barn Artisan Food Village, where son Andrew has joined Sue. All the cheeses are as unique in flavour as they are recognisable in sizing and brand image, the Celtic Cross having quickly established them as county classics.

Whalesborough Farm is still home to the Proudfoots and Sue, not content with a singular pursuit, still runs a smallholding on the farm, the range and number of animals exceeding the tally in the Domesday Book. Its farming tradition continues, embellished by a new chapter.

KELTIC GOLD

 AGE AT RELEASE
6 weeks

STYLE
Semi Hard, Washed Rind

RENNET
Vegetarian

MILK TYPE
Cow: Jersey, Geurnsey, Ayrshire, Fresian

 350g, 1.3kg

 Small Drum, Drum

TASTING NOTE
A high-tone game musk on the rind softens on the palate to straw, seed and field mushroom with a citric thread at the core.

WHERE TO BUY
Via the website or wholesalers and cheesemongers countrywide. See web for details.

WHAT TO DRINK
Off-dry whites, light fruity reds, malty ale, ciders.

MISS MUFFET

AGE AT RELEASE
4 weeks

STYLE
Semi Soft

RENNET
Vegetarian

MILK TYPE
Cow: As for Keltic
Gold

300g, 1.3kg

Small Drum, Drum

TASTING NOTE

Semi-strong, clean and tangy lactic core with light white game notes strengthening to spice and morels closer to the rind.

WHERE TO BUY

Via the website or wholesalers and cheesemongers countrywide. See web for details.

WHAT TO DRINK

Aromatic off-dry whites, light chilled reds, cider and hoppy ales.

NANNY MUFFET

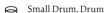
AGE AT RELEASE
6 weeks

STYLE
Semi Hard

RENNET
Vegetarian

MILK TYPE
Goat

300g, 1.3kg

Small Drum, Drum

TASTING NOTE

Light leather and dusty stone aromas threaded with wild mushroom at the rind, and a balanced palate of complex milled seed, warm hay and yeasty bread at the core. Outstanding.

WHERE TO BUY

Via the website or wholesalers and cheesemongers countrywide. See web for details.

WHAT TO DRINK

Semi-sweet whites, medium-bodied reds, malty ales, off-dry cider.

Clare and Tom Noblet

WHIN YEATS

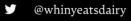

WHIN YEATS

◉ HUTTON ROOF, CUMBRIA

———————

The Whin Yeats Dairy is another source of delight for the cheese lover, born of hardship for the farmer.

Tom and Clare Noblet farm in partnership with the owners of Whin Yeats' picturesque Cumbrian hill farm. In 2014 it was apparent that their pedigree Holstein Friesians were at risk if they allowed the future to be dictated by fluctuating milk prices, so they built a dairy and sought alternative returns from their low-output herd.

Nowadays bulk milk prices are largely set to international market levels. Increasingly, in order to remain competitive in the UK, as well as growing the size of a herd, maximum output is sought from each cow. This often leads to cows with shorter lifespans, some as little as six years. At Whin Yeats the herd is closed (in that all breeding is done on-farm) and some of the cows are over 16 years old.

With the encouragement and assistance of Andy Swinscoe at the Courtyard Dairy, an inspirational cheesemonger in Settle, Tom and Claire have helped rekindle the farmhouse Wensleydale tradition with their Fellstone and the older Farmhouse cheeses. Though made between the Lake District and the Dales, they are as Wensleydale would have been before World War Two, from unpasteurised milk and cloth-bound, safeguarding the particular characteristics introduced by the bacteria and moulds native to their pasture-filled valley between Hutton Roof and the craggy Farlton Knott.

In addition to cows they farm a flock of Rough Fell sheep, native to the area, as well as pigs and hens, all enhancing the farm's viability. It is such diversity that seems the only choice left for artisans wishing to avoid more intensive methods of farming. As for the cheese, the benefit to the consumer is immediately apparent and, as is so often the case, the little extra asked for the cheese doesn't do justice to the painstaking cost of production.

FARMHOUSE

AGE AT RELEASE

4 months

STYLE

Hard

RENNET

Animal

MILK TYPE

Cow: Holstein
Friesian

3.5kg

Drum

TASTING NOTE

Clotted cream, cashew and hay notes from the even,
semi-elastic core, and a giving palate of lemon and
floral flavours, leading to more stone mineral and
bacon smoke characters on the rind. Outstanding.

WHERE TO BUY

See web for details.

WHAT TO DRINK

Aromatic off-dry whites, light chilled reds, cider and
hoppy ales.

Roger Longman

WHITE LAKE CHEESE

WHITE LAKE CHEESE

Few wouldn't rank White Lake among the cheese world's top innovators. Lesser cheesemakers would require convalescence after a week trying to manage a dairy with twenty-eight unique recipes to its repertoire, but Peter Humphries and Roger Longman have crafted a business that pairs inventive cheesemaking and high-grade milk to produce a consistency unsurpassed from a range so broad.

Roger grew up at Bagborough Farm on the eastern tip of the Somerset Levels, verdant pastureland synonymous with Cheddar production. Even though his parents and grandparents made the area's signature cheese, it held little interest for Roger. Instead he started a career in engineering, only returning to the farm after Cheddar production had ceased due to the commercial pressures faced by supplying the block Cheddar market. The farm retained the dairy cows for milk, but the cheesemaking renaissance began with goat's milk when, in 2001, Roger introduced a small herd to the farm. His uncle made a little cheese but the White Lake business partnership got underway in 2004 when Roger met Peter, a former cheesemaker at Bath Soft Cheese.

The desire to innovate was there from the outset, Peter deciding to create cheeses that were little seen in the UK. It was trial and error at first, 'working by feel' to no strict recipe, at first allowing each cheese its seasonal expressions due to the fluctuation in milk composition. The pair trialled each new cheese at farmers' markets, only approaching wholesalers when they felt they really 'understood' the cheese. From this point they could work in harmony with the milk and tweak the recipe throughout the year to produce consistently high quality.

Expansion in 2008 drew Roger into dairy duties, the variety having kindled a passion absent for Cheddar making. The dairy now has 800 goats producing milk for 85% of the cheese that White Lake makes. It arrives in the dairy warm from the barns and is processed unpasteurised with minimal handling to retain the delicate sweet-milk character of the cheeses. Although the farm's cows have moved on, White Lake buys in a little Guernsey cow milk, as well as sheep's milk, from local farms for some of its cheeses.

The organic and self-confessed 'chaotic' nature of their business belies a firm understanding of what constitutes success in the artisan cheese world: originality and quality derived from a purity of source milk. Having mastered this, the pair can concentrate on consistency and allow the flow of awards themselves to promote and market the range all it needs.

Goat breeds: Alpine, Saanen, Toggenburg

E V E

 AGE AT RELEASE
3 weeks

STYLE
Soft, Vine Leaf Wrapped

RENNET
Vegetarian

MILK TYPE
Goat: See notes.

 125g

 Small Drum

TASTING NOTE
A cider-washed, vine wrapped creation that allows the fresh creamy paste to the fore with grass, citrus and a gently goaty rice pudding note, with mushrrom and vine-herbal notes towards the rind. Outstanding.

WHERE TO BUY
Wholesalers and cheesemongers countrywide. See web for details.

WHAT TO DRINK
Rich sparkling, aromatic whites, medium-bodied reds, off-dry cider & ale.

SOMERSET SOLSTICE

AGE AT RELEASE
4 weeks

STYLE
Soft, Washed Rind

RENNET
Vegetarian

MILK TYPE
Cow: Guernsey

220g

Small Drum

TASTING NOTE

A subtle and three-tiered cheese with a lighly saline, singed cream and citrus core, chanterelle mushroom creamy under-rind and a nutmeg spice and winged game rind. Outstanding.

WHERE TO BUY

Wholesalers and cheesemongers countrywide. See web for details.

WHAT TO DRINK

Off-dry sparkling, medium-bodied whites, medium-bodied reds, off-dry cider & session ale.

DRIFTWOOD

AGE AT RELEASE
3 weeks

STYLE
Fresh, Bloomy

RENNET
Vegetarian

MILK TYPE
Goat: See notes.

215g

Log

TASTING NOTE

An even, lactic core with elegant goat milk, citrus and parsley notes, turning to fresh apple and mushroom on the rind. Outstanding.

WHERE TO BUY

Wholesalers and cheesemongers countrywide. See web for details.

WHAT TO DRINK

Sparkling, crisp whites, chilled light reds, dry ciders, citric ales.

TOR

AGE AT RELEASE
3 weeks

STYLE
Fresh, Bloomy

RENNET
Vegetarian

MILK TYPE
Goat: See notes.

200g

Truncated Pyramid

TASTING NOTE
A moreish smooth-pasted cheese with clean lime, cream and fresh grass flavours at the core, richening towards the rind with notes of toasted mushroom. Outstanding.

WHERE TO BUY
Wholesalers and cheesemongers countrywide. See web for details.

WHAT TO DRINK
Sparkling, crisp whites, chilled light reds, dry ciders, citric ales.

PAVE COBBLE

AGE AT RELEASE
3 weeks

STYLE
Soft, Bloomy

RENNET
Vegetarian

MILK TYPE
Sheep

200g

Truncated Pyramid

TASTING NOTE
A ripe parcel of lanolin-scented lemon, mixed herb and gently saline cream at the core, with an intriguing basket of mixed mushroom on the rind. Outstanding.

WHERE TO BUY
Wholesalers and cheesemongers countrywide. See web for details.

WHAT TO DRINK
Sparkling, crisp whites, chilled light reds, dry ciders, citric ales.

RACHEL

 AGE AT RELEASE

3 months

STYLE

Semi Hard

RENNET

Vegetarian

MILK TYPE

Goat: See notes.

 2kg

 Ammonite

TASTING NOTE

Delicate rind with a range of musk and dry earth notes not to be missed. On the palate a variety of flavours eminates from the semi-hard crumble: fresh grass, milled seed, rice pudding and caramel, strengthening towards the rind with died meat and trompette de mort flavours. Exceptional.

WHERE TO BUY

Wholesalers and cheesemongers countrywide. See web for details.

WHAT TO DRINK

Off-dry sparkling, medium-bodied whites, medium-bodied reds, off-dry cider & session ale.

Julie Cheyney

WHITE WOOD DAIRY

:camera: @st.judecheese

:bird: @stjudecheese

:calendar: www.stjudecheese.com

WHITE WOOD DAIRY

◎ BUNGAY, SUFFOLK

———————

A dairymaid in her teens and married to a farmer for 30 years, Julie Cheyney realised her dream of becoming a cheesemaker when in 2005 she established Hampshire Cheeses with Stacey Hedges and helped bring Tunworth into being.

Success there spurred her to start her own business. After two years travelling to cheese regions and a collaboration with the team at Neal's Yard Dairy, her slow-make lactic cheese, St Jude, was born at White Wood Dairy on the Hampshire Downs. As with Tunworth, the quality of her cheese fast attracted praise and awards, but Julie's perfectionism soon led her to pastures new when she heard of an opportunity to make cheese from the milk of a herd of Montbéliarde cows on Stow Fen in Suffolk. As one of the breeds responsible for Comté and Vacherin in the Jura, Julie knew that Montbéliarde milk would be ideal for her soft St Marcellin-inspired cheese, and the high animal welfare at Fen Farm, home to Baron Bigod, well suited her ethos.

St Cera, a washed-rind version of St Jude, was added to her offering in 2017. To make cheese from raw milk is paramount for Julie, believing it not only best for health but also imparting a truer expression of the environment from which it comes. Until 2018 Julie shared her make room with the cheesemakers at Fen Farm, but a larger adjacent dairy constructed in 2018 for Baron Bigod has given Julie the old make room to herself and the opportunity to develop more creations. Both St Jude and St Cera have won the Specialist Cheesemakers Association's James Aldridge Trophy for raw milk cheese, a unique double for any cheesemaker. Voted on exclusively by cheesemaking peers, it's the pinnacle for a British crafter of curd.

ST JUDE

 AGE AT RELEASE
2 weeks

STYLE
Soft, Bloomy

RENNET
Animal

MILK TYPE
Cow: Montbéliarde

 120g

 Small Drum

TASTING NOTE

A pretty rind with a white morel wrinkle. The nose has fresh grass and field mushroom aromas and the palate clean flavours of gently salted cream and seared cep. Outstanding.

WHERE TO BUY

Farm shop, online or wholesalers and cheesemongers countrywide. See web for details.

WHAT TO DRINK

Sparkling, aromatic whites, light reds, hoppy ale and cider.

ST CERA

AGE AT RELEASE
3 weeks

STYLE
Soft, Washed Rind

RENNET
Animal

MILK TYPE
Cow: Montbéliarde

120g

Small Drum

TASTING NOTE

A pretty rind with a white morel wrinkle and some light blueing. The nose has fresh grass and field mushroom aromas and the palate gives clean flavours of gently salted cream, seared cep and summer flowers. Richer and porcini-like closer to the rind. Exceptional.

WHERE TO BUY

Farm shop or wholesalers and cheesemongers countrywide. See web for details.

WHAT TO DRINK

Off-dry sparkling or white, mead, ale.

Philip Walton

WILDES CHEESE

As far as farming goes, North London may not be a match for the lush pastures of Somerset or the Cheshire Plain, but since 2012 it has been the source of some great cheese.

The organic milk for Wildes Cheese travels sixty miles north from a small, low-yielding herd of cows at the Northiam Dairy in Rye, Sussex, to where the magic happens on an industrial unit within the urban enclave of Tottenham. Before founding the business, Philip Walton had considered leaving the community that had embraced him since his move from Cyprus at the age of 16, to be in a rural setting. This, he felt, would enable him to live out his passion for home cheesemaking after leaving a career in management consultancy. But before uprooting from an area that he held dear, an idea struck him: the grain for London's new-wave brewers, bakers and distillers was brought in, so why not milk for his cheese?

At a time soon after the riots he was keen to be a part of the area's regeneration, so he decided to stay. The first year was largely taken up with trials in a unit not much larger than a garage, but a move to larger premises followed, which allowed more than just a space to make enough cheese but also a venue to interact with the customers who would buy it. School visits, courses and events now form a significant part of the business, making use of an asset on the doorstep denied many a cheesemaker: an abundance of cosmopolitan palates eager to taste something new.

It is a sense of the new that is at the heart of the business. From the outset Wildes resolved not to follow set recipes, and each of their cheeses has a twist or more from any classical style, be it soft, blue or hard. Now with husband Keith Sides helping to power the cheesemaking, there are over thirty creations in their portfolio, a core of eight available at most times, all distinctly Wildes, using a wide array of starter cultures and moulds and aligning them with make-methods that shun conformity.

Once a month they create a new cheese and call it Brian. Some are the result of customer requests from their bespoke cheesemaking service, but most are born of a desire to break new ground. 'If it's honest, decent and legal, we'll make it,' states Philip, championing a free-spirited philosophy that has garnered Michelin-starred clients both rural and urban.

ALEXANDRA

 AGE AT RELEASE
12 weeks

STYLE
Semi Hard

RENNET
Vegetarian

MILK TYPE
Cow: Jersey

 2kg

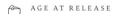 Drum

TASTING NOTE
A friable core with clean floral notes and hints of crème caramel, richening towards the rind where the flavours become those of mushroom broth. Outstanding.

WHERE TO BUY
Via the website or wholesalers and cheesemongers in London. See web for details.

WHAT TO DRINK
Aromatic off-dry whites, light chilled reds, cider and hoppy ales.

BABY BLUE

AGE AT RELEASE
3 weeks

STYLE
Semi Soft, Blue

RENNET
Vegetarian

MILK TYPE
Cow: Jersey

 350g

Disk

TASTING NOTE

A pretty, mottled rind emitting savoury mushroom and game notes with a rich core palate of flavours: toffee apple, chanterelle, and dried orchard fruit in singed cream. Outstanding.

WHERE TO BUY

Via the website or wholesalers and cheesemongers in London. See web for details.

WHAT TO DRINK

Rich reds, tawny port, sherry, winter ale and sweet cider.

LONDONSHIRE

AGE AT RELEASE
2 weeks

STYLE
Soft, Bloomy

RENNET
Vegetarian

MILK TYPE
Cow: Jersey

 220g

Disk

TASTING NOTE

A thick mushroom-crunch through the rind leads to a sweet cream palate with flavours of salted macadamia and field mushroom.

WHERE TO BUY

Via the website or wholesalers and cheesemongers in London. See web for details.

WHAT TO DRINK

Sparkling, aromatic whites, light reds, hoppy ale and cider.

Robin and Carla Betts

WINTERDALE SHAW

🔲 @winterdalecheesemakers

🐦 @winterdalekent

🗓 www.winterdale.co.uk

WINTERDALE SHAW

At the end of a twenty-mile dale that curves northward to the Thames Estuary sits a wood-framed Kentish barn atop a chalk cave. To the uninitiated it's a piece of Platt House Farm as ancient as the surrounding oaks.

When, in 2000, Robin and Carla Betts settled on the idea of cheesemaking to safeguard the future of the family's 500-year farming tradition (another threatened by low milk prices) they might have been tempted to go for a quick solution, such as erecting a temporary building to make an early-ripening cheese that would yield early cashflow. Instead they raised the funds needed to carve down into the chalk subsoil to create a cave to house traditional British cheeses that would require long-term ageing. They knew this would grant the maturing cheeses moulds unique to their location, adding to flavour and complexity, but above all they thought that the cave in time would pay for itself, removing the costs of artificial humidity and temperature control. The cave dug, they constructed the barn above out of green oak to a traditional template, realising it needed to be a draw, a venue where people could connect with the cheese, the shop and viewing gallery wise investments that would retain profits otherwise lost to wholesale.

The milk comes from the family's dairy on the hillside opposite. Around it the lush fields that see more than their share of rainfall are unlike the Wealden clay to the south, their porous chalky subsoil capable of absorbing much of its excess, thus allowing the herd extended access to grazing and reducing the need for winter feed. Once the milk arrives at the barn, still warm from the cow and unpasteurised, the processes are gravity-fed. Whilst beneficial to quality in minimising unnecessary handling which can damage milk, it also saves energy and lessens the environmental impact of their business, something at the heart of the Carla and Robin's ethos. A ground source heat pump, solar panels and a wind turbine have since contributed to make the farm carbon neutral.

This unusually joined-up and long-term approach has created a community hub and, importantly for the farm, has enabled direct sales, a real bonus in an industry with slim margins. It seems that at Winterdale Shaw the future lies in honouring the old ways.

WINTERDALE SHAW

 AGE AT RELEASE
10 months

STYLE
Hard

RENNET
Animal

MILK TYPE
Cow: Holstein
Friesian

 10kg

 Large Drum

TASTING NOTE

A hearty mouthful packed with balanced and changing flavours of crème brulée, baked orchard fruit and cep, with a stone-mineral and warm bark rind. Outstanding.

WHERE TO BUY

Farm shop or wholesalers and cheesemongers countrywide. See web for details.

WHAT TO DRINK

Sweet whites, rich reds, tawny port, malty ale, strong cider.

Emily Davies

WOODBRIDGE FARM

@dorsetbluevinney

@dorsetbluevinney

www.dorsetblue.com

WOODBRIDGE FARM

Tired of being restricted by milk quotas and beholden to the bureaucracy of supplying a wholesale commodity he felt no one valued, in 1980 dairy farmer Mike Davies turned to cheese.

Once a cheesemaker by training he decided he would have to make something different to stand out from the typical Somerset output of Cheddar. He struck on the idea of re-creating Dorset Blue Vinney, a cheese once ubiquitous in Dorset farmhouse production that had sadly died out.

There were several factors in its demise. The first was the Milk Marketing Board's inception in 1933. Providing a ready buyer of farm milk, it turned many makers of this tricky blue away from the onerous task of producing it. The war took the style to its grave with the ban during rationing. Few took up the style thereafter. Traditionally made from soured milk that had been skimmed for milk or butter, modern methods of skimming left too little butterfat to make a quality cheese, so the style became overlooked. By the 1960s, apart from a few cheeses passed off as Blue Vinney that were in fact unscrupulously mislabelled examples of downgraded Stilton, the style was no more.

Mike began by making the cheeses in his farmhouse kitchen and maturing them in the family's pantry. The precocious moulds unfortunately found their way onto any surface that would support them, from walls to cornflakes, so ageing was soon moved to a converted cow byre. In 1984 the first Dorset Blue Vinny (Woodbridge Farm dropped the 'e') cheeses came to market.

The term 'vinney' comes from the old English 'vinew' meaning mould. The cheese, being lower in fat and crumbly, would have easily turned mouldy, something said to have been encouraged in blues by dragging a mouldy harness through the milk or leaving cheeses next to muddy boots.

The milk for Dorset Blue Vinny, after skimming, is inoculated with starter and then rennet and penicillin is added. The curd is cut two hours later and left overnight before the whey is drained off. The curds are then ground, salted and fed into moulds. The cheeses are then rubbed-up, sealing the fissures from the air, thus preventing any mould forming early. They are spiked at around four weeks later when the desired level of ripeness has been reached. The result is a blue with fine veining, milder in strength than Stilton.

In 1998, further to the discovery of out-of-county blue cheese being sold as Dorset Blue Vinny, the farm obtained a PGI for Dorset Blue Vinny, helping to protect its reputation.

DORSET BLUE VINNY

 AGE AT RELEASE

5 months

STYLE

Semi Hard, Blue

RENNET

Animal

MILK TYPE

Cow: Holstein
Friesian

 6kg

 Cylinder

TASTING NOTE

Sweet and sweaty macadamia, spice and dried apricot
on the nose, with a high-blue palate over creamy, malty
and wild mushroom notes at the core, and a darker
rind: seared pigeon breast and spice.

WHERE TO BUY

Via the website or wholesalers and cheesemongers
countrywide. See web for details.

WHAT TO DRINK

Rich reds, port, sweet whites and medium cider.

Dave Bartlett

WOOTTON
ORGANIC DAIRY

www.woottondairy.com

WOOTTON ORGANIC DAIRY

The Wootton Organic Dairy is a paradigm of passion. In 1969 the Bartlett family moved to Sunnyside Farm's rolling acres on the Somerset Levels overlooking Glastonbury Tor. From then until the late 90s beef was the business, the ancient Red Devon breed providing the locality with rich cuts of meat. When sons Dave and James Bartlett returned to the farm in 1999 the smallholding needed to produce more. The decision to milk sheep was taken, but a few calculations showed that the tiny yields and seasonal nature of the milk would little further their ambition, so the idea of cheesemaking was settled upon.

At the time Mary Holbrook, a post-war pioneer of sheep's milk cheesemaking, was shifting her focus from sheep to goats. The Bartletts took the opportunity to purchase Mary's recipe for Little Ryding, her popular bloomy-rinded soft cheese. The boys converted a stone outhouse into a dairy and, following a few lessons from Mary, began making the cheese true to the original but with the microflora of their own pastures, diverse in herbage and spring wildflowers, giving their cheese unique characters. The farm had always been run along organic principles and it was something Dave and James chose to make official when they took over. They believe organic milk not only improves the quality of their cheese by avoiding unwanted residues, but it also enhances the complexity of flavour due to the preserved abundance of microflora.

Other cheeses followed Little Ryding, including Millstone, a hard Manchego-style, and Wootton White, a fresh Feta-style. The seasonal nature of sheep's milk (lactation being difficult to accomplish year-round in a flock) led the pair to start making cheese from the milk of a local Jersey herd. In 2001 they switched to their own Jersey milk when they added nine cows to the farm's stock.

They now make eight cheeses, about 450 a week from sheep's, cow's and mixed-milk, as well as yoghurt, exclusively using every drop of the farm's output. It's no mean feat lambing 300 ewes, caring for cows, milking twice a day in season, as well as making cheese and yoghurt, and then finding time to sell them in person to eager buyers at local farmers' markets. It's not a rosy path to riches either. It's a dedicated and driven pursuit which requires every family member to share and commit to a passion for the product, and that's a rarity as scarce as the Bartletts' cheeses.

DUMPLING

 AGE AT RELEASE
10 days

STYLE
Soft, Bloomy

RENNET
Vegetarian

MILK TYPE
Sheep: Freisland, Poll Dorset

150g

Button

TASTING NOTE
A wrinkled rind with mineral and light game notes leads to a crisp, lactic palate with fresh seed and citric characters.

WHERE TO BUY
Wholesalers and retailers locally. See website for details.

WHAT TO DRINK
Sparkling, crisp whites, chilled reds & dry cider.

LITTLE RYDING

 AGE AT RELEASE
3 weeks

STYLE
Soft, Bloomy

RENNET
Vegetarian

MILK TYPE
Sheep: Freisland, Poll Dorset

 220g

 Small Disk, Disk

TASTING NOTE

Clean core with flavours of citrus, cream and floral notes, enveloped in a springy rind with field mushroom and white game flavours. Outstanding.

WHERE TO BUY

Wholesalers and retailers locally. See website for details.

WHAT TO DRINK

Sparkling, aromatic whites, light chilled reds, cider & crisp ale.

THE CAMPAIGN FOR
BRITISH ARTISAN CHEESE

WHAT IS THE FUTURE FOR BRITISH ARTISAN CHEESE?

When we began cheesemaking at Gimblett Cheese it was with the knowledge that British artisan produce was on the rise. Since starting our tasting events business back in 1997 we had witnessed the increase in English sparkling wine producers, British micro-breweries and small batch distillers, and, thinking that artisan cheese might be similarly set for exponential growth, we sought to benefit from any potential upsurge in demand by becoming producers.

What we have found suggests to me that whilst the artisan cheese industry is in a stronger position today than it has been at any time since the war, it is still a fraction of that of other European countries. Furthermore, due to the consolidation of our dairy milk industry, as well as other inhibiting factors, time is running out to grow the industry.

When visiting cheesemakers for the preparation of the Guide, I wanted to know whether my suppositions were well founded and if the hurdles we had to clear to become cheesemakers were unique, so I took the opportunity to canvass their opinions. The breadth of response and the depth of passion I encountered have convinced me that there is much still to be done to nurse our artisan cheese industry beyond infancy.

There would be subject matter enough to dedicate an entire book to addressing these issues, but I will convey my thoughts here in summary, in the hope of stimulating further discussion and promoting awareness of the challenges faced by those who strive to bring artisan cheese to your tables.

HAS BRITAIN MORE CHEESES THAN FRANCE?

Not even close. This oft-mooted marketing line I had swallowed prior to a little research is deeply misleading. When first I compiled a list of qualifying cheeses I soon realised my supposition that we had as many cheeses as France was nonsense and I felt embarrassed at having mentioned this fiction at our tastings. According to the French ministry of agriculture, France has over 2000 commercial cheesemakers and there are probably many more selling cheese from smallholdings or at local markets. We have around 300 cheesemakers in total.

It was with a sense of relief that I found I wasn't the only one who'd been fooled. Many of the cheese guides I researched told a similar story, some saying that we have more cheeses than France, others more cheesemakers. Online I found national newspaper articles echoing the same, as were some expert sources. I asked the Specialist Cheesemakers Association how this delusion might have arisen. The answer was that it probably came from a statement made by a prominent expert in the 2000s that England has more styles of cheese than France, claiming that our desire to experiment has resulted in a wider range of different recipes. This speaks to the fact that many French cheesemakers make their cheese to a style, or recipe, prescribed by a Protected Designation of Origin (PDO) or similar. Whilst this may or may not be the case (as there are nearly a thousand cheesemakers in France working outside PDO restrictions whose styles could equally be said to be unique), it's one thing to be justifiably proud of what we produce, but quite another to project a skewed image of a seemingly thriving industry that needs little help. When faced with the ranks of imported artisan cheese on our shelves, why should the consumer feel the need to select one of the few British offerings if our industry is already world-beating? Though the quality of our best artisan cheeses is comparable with the world's best, our artisan cheese industry isn't, yet.

WHY GROW THE ARTISAN CHEESE INDUSTRY?

1. FOR FLAVOUR

Highly processed cheesemaking milk from bulk sources provides less diverse microflora leading to a restriction in the variety of flavours. This usually results in bland cheese, rather than the infinitely preferable richly-flavoured cheeses made possible by carefully handled milk from pasture-grazed, low yielding livestock.

2. FOR HEALTH

Microbially diverse cheesemaking milk leads to richer concentrations of bacteria and enzymes beneficial to our microbiome. Better for our guts.

3. FOR OUR COMMUNITIES

Locally owned and operated farms keep knowledge, tradition, skills, employment and revenue in the community.

4. FOR OUR COWS

Milk produced for artisan cheese does not have volume as its key driver, so animals naturally yield less and live longer lives. Keeping our cows in pastures and out of factories also improves livestock welfare.

5. FOR OUR HERITAGE

Most of our 'heritage' cheeses, such as Cheddar or Red Leicestershire, are now mass-produced and have become a shadow of the cheeses that made their names great. More producers making cheese to artisan methods will restore the potential of these styles and raise global awareness of the great heritage of British cheese.

WHAT'S STOPPING US GROWING THE INDUSTRY?

1. AVAILABILITY OF ARTISAN CHEESE-GRADE MILK

Official Agriculture and Horticulture Development Board figures show that between 1997 and 2017 the number of UK milk-producing dairies fell from 35,741 to 12,960. That's an average of three dairies a day closing down.

We're producing more milk than ever, but on bigger farms and from commercial feed. This means more mundane milk as a starting point for potential cheesemakers. Even if the rate of closure slows to half the current rate in the face of crippling low milk prices, we would be left with as few as 5000 dairies by 2030. That may still sound like a lot, but it will be the smaller, pasture-grazed, lower-yielding herds and the smaller breeds that will disappear first, leaving the aspiring artisan cheesemaker little to work with.

Time is running out. We have less than ten years to turn the industry around.

If, as a nation, there was the will then we could transform some of these dairies into viable cheese producers, taking us from 300 to 1,000 artisan cheese producers by 2030.

The answer: connecting dairy farmers with budding new cheesemakers via industry bodies such as the NFU and the Agriculture and Horticulture Development Board.

2. MILK PRODUCERS CONSTRAINED BY THE MILK WHOLESALE MARKET

Many small dairy farmers are tied to sole supply contracts with large wholesalers. This stifles diversification and the diminishing milk margins lead to the demise of the small farm.

The answer: Milk contracts need to be more flexible, allowing small farms to diversify in order to grow their revenues.

3. KNOWLEDGE OF HOW TO CREATE DISTINCT ARTISAN CHEESE

Aspiring new cheesemakers need to craft cheeses that can be distinguished from mass-market offerings, and thus guidance and training by individuals who understand the artisan market. The route to market will be easier for those who select a niche and make their cheese to quality levels that customers can't ignore and the mass market cannot compete with. Artisan cheesemaking should not be the adaptation of mass-market ideas to the small scale. Therein lies only failure.

The answer: see our recommended courses and industry bodies in the Resources page on the Gimblett Cheese website. *www.gimblettcheese.co.uk*

4. AN UNDERSTANDING OF CHEESE BUSINESS MATTERS FOR THE NEW CHEESEMAKER

Whilst there are many good cheesemaking courses in the UK, and a body to promote excellence in artisan cheesemaking, the artisan cheese industry lacks a collective or mentoring system to support the fledgling cheesemaker with guidance in marketplace access and business structure.

The answer: a business of cheesemaking collective or panel of experts who can be called upon to assist a new artisan cheesemaker.

5. A DIFFICULT ROUTE TO MARKET FOR THE ARTISAN PRODUCER

Supermarkets find small producers inefficient to deal with and small producers find supermarkets bureaucratically heavy-handed and, with few exceptions, not at all interested in promoting regionality. In short, they are a fundamental mismatch and probably not the vehicle for growing the artisan cheese industry.

Farmers' markets can work for an artisan producer, and many cheesemakers have built their businesses upon them, but after a boom in the early 2000s, many such markets are struggling.

The answer: More delicatessens and dedicated cheesemongers, crucially allowing the public to sample what's on offer before buying. Knowledge and enthusiasm are paramount. There is no point in a delicatessen buying bland cheese, in or aping the range or methods of a supermarket. There is a huge difference between great and boring cheese, and the customer needs to be helped to taste it. There is good business to be had for the innovative and approachable cheesemonger.

6. LACK OF AWARENESS IN THE MARKET

This is the one thing that most cheesemakers referenced when asked for their chief difficulty. The British public are not as food-aware (or experimental) as other European nations. We are now more aware when it comes to wine and other artisan produce, but it seems that our awareness of cheese is still lagging. How do we change that?

PUBLIC AWARENESS

A group of industry experts has formed the Academy of Cheese, a not-for-profit organisation that is at the forefront of raising awareness within the food industry as well as the public. If you are in the business of cooking with or serving artisan cheese, its courses will set you apart from the ill-informed. If you love simply love cheese, they will enhance your enjoyment many-fold.

www.academyofcheese.org

TELEVISION

Food on television is focused upon cookery and though some television chefs have been good at highlighting individual producers and their cheeses, the recipe is always paramount. A little more light needs to be shone upon the creators of our diverse and fabulous cheeses as well as how they came about.

RESTAURANTS

When made to high standards, artisan cheese has the potential to provide as sensuous and complex a flavour experience as the finest wine. It is also the only single-ingredient course offered on a restaurant menu. Yet, even in many fine establishments, the diner is often given little or no choice and even less information, with menus often stating only a generic term, such as Cheddar, Stilton or Brie. This is the equivalent of having a wine list indicating only Red, White or Rosé, something we stopped seeing in the 1980s.

The answer: cheese menus with named regional producers, a tasting note and other information, such as the cheese's age. Give cheese the respect afforded to wine and bring our menus into the new millennium.

There is no single simple fix for the industry, rather a series of changes to tackle together. And whilst change is daunting, the thing we should fear more is the status quo.

Please follow the Campaign for British Artisan Cheese via @francisgimblett on YouTube, Instagram and Twitter.